Tough Conversations
with the
Heart of Jesus

RICHARD TILLER

WESTBOW·
PRESS
A DIVISION OF THOMAS NELSON
& ZONDERVAN

Scriptures taken from the Holy Bible, New International Version®,
NIV®. Copyright © 1973, 1978, 1984, 2011 by Biblica, Inc.™ Used
by permission of Zondervan. All rights reserved worldwide. www.
zondervan.com The "NIV" and "New International Version"
are trademarks registered in the United States Patent and
Trademark Office by Biblica, Inc.™ All rights reserved.

WestBow Press books may be ordered through booksellers or by contacting:

WestBow Press
A Division of Thomas Nelson & Zondervan
1663 Liberty Drive
Bloomington, IN 47403
www.westbowpress.com
1 (866) 928-1240

ISBN: 978-1-4908-3450-4 (sc)
ISBN: 978-1-4908-3451-1 (hc)
ISBN: 978-1-4908-3449-8 (e)

Library of Congress Control Number: 2014907178

Printed in the United States of America.

WestBow Press rev. date: 5/9/2014

Contents

CHAPTER 1

Opportunities

He Was Doomed

Andy was trouble from the first day. His parents had sent him away to boarding school when he was in tenth grade. I never learned much of his story, but I knew his life at home was hard.

I was a senior when I met him. As prefect of the corridor down which Andy lived, I tried to reach out to him, but he blew me off. He wanted no help. He wanted no friends. All he seemed to want was trouble. He treated everyone badly, and they gave it back. He racked up a lot of demerits, and he had the worst grades in his class. His survival at the school looked short term. Maybe that's the way he wanted it. All I could figure was that failure was his revenge for being sent there against his will. But after three months, he was still there.

I found myself having less and less contact with Andy. There was something about him I liked. I wanted him to make it, but I was losing interest in him. I just wanted to contain the collateral damage to the rest of the corridor caused by his self-destruction; any more involvement with him didn't seem worth the effort. I didn't anticipate something wonderful was about to happen—for Andy and for me.

He Wasn't Doomed After All

One day, another boy from the corridor came to my room and said Andy wanted to see me in his room. He was summoning me. *What's with this?* I asked myself. I found him at his desk. I closed the door and sat on his bed. "What's up?" I asked. He opened his desk drawer and took out a pack of cigarettes and an ashtray. He was trying to get suspended. The way it worked was that the first time a student got caught smoking he was suspended; the second time he was expelled. This would be his first offense. The second one would set him free. Andy had finally come up with the perfect plan—self-destruction without hurting anyone else.

He struck a match, lit up, took a long drag, and closed his eyes. He smiled to dramatize his enjoyment of the moment.

"You don't have a choice now," he said. "You've got to suspend me."

"Fair enough. I guess you've got me over a barrel here. I was really rooting for you to make it. I thought you had a lot of offer, and I still do. But I guess it's too late. Enjoy your cigarette. We can chat until you're done."

He looked confused, as though he was feeling an uncomfortable mix of victory and disappointment. "What do you mean I have a lot to offer?"

"I mean you have a lot to offer," I said, "and now it's all going to be wasted."

"What're you talking about?" His tone was mostly sneering, but it also held a trace of curiosity.

"Well, you're a good-looking guy, everybody knows you've got plenty of brains, and you have a cool way about you when you're not being a jackass. If you tried just a little, you could be a guy people wanted to hang around with—and for the right reasons too. I don't know you that well, Andy, but I think there's a lot of good in your heart. I always have. And that's the truth." It was the truth.

Andy began to cry.

"Did I insult you with that compliment?" I asked with a slight laugh. It was more nervousness than humor. "I know what a badass you are." My laugh became more comfortable. A little laugh of his own worked its way through his sobbing. He laughed and cried intermittently for half a minute or so. Finally, he said, "That's the kindest thing anyone's ever said to me."

He set his cigarette in the ashtray. I reached over and put it out.

"How about if you let other people see the real Andy?" I said.

"What about the cigarette?" he asked.

"What cigarette?"

And that was it.

The conversation could have gone on for a while, but it didn't. He said thanks for talking and for giving him another chance. I told him I was glad to have him on the corridor and to have him as a friend.

It Was a Game Changer

We talked a lot more that year, always about the present or the near future, never about the past or the distant future. As the year progressed, Andy became a role model, a fellow others wanted as a friend, and a positive influence. He became an outstanding student, even top in his class for a couple of grading periods. His transformation was a joy to watch.

I had no positive feelings about meeting with Andy when I entered his room the day we talked. It never occurred to me any good would come of it for either of us. I just figured it would be a tough conversation. I didn't see it as an opportunity until after it was over.

I lost touch with Andy after that year. I don't know what happened to him after he got home. I know his transformation was profound, but I don't know if it was permanent. What I do know is that I was transformed by that conversation, profoundly and permanently. My transformation wasn't as visible as Andy's at first; it took longer to take shape, but it had a huge impact on what I believe about tough conversations today, forty-six years later. Over time, I learned to embrace tough conversations as potentially transformational. Thinking about that potential gives me a joy that overcomes my fear and anxiety.

Then Came a Bigger Game Changer

The school I attended with Andy was a Christian boarding school. My upbringing had familiarized me with

Christianity before, and that was one of the reasons I went there. I'm grateful for that five-year period. Jesus was an influence in my life during those years, but I didn't fully embrace the Christian faith until thirteen years later. Yet as I look back on that conversation with Andy, I see the presence of Jesus at work.

In college, I drifted far away from Jesus and remained spiritually adrift until I was thirty. But Jesus never drifted away from me. Looking back, I see how He remained present in my heart during tough conversations. The blessings that have resulted from tough conversations throughout my adult life I owe to His love. The times when conversations went south were times when I closed my heart to Him.

After college, I went into new-home sales. I discovered a grace in my ability to tell the truth that needed to be told when it needed to be told in my relationships with customers. But this grace was not always consistent. The times I drifted from sincerity backfired disastrously, which got me back on track quickly. I had a good career in sales, and I believe that was due largely to my desire to have productive conversations with a sincere heart no matter how difficult those conversations were.

By the time I entered management, the way I embraced Jesus was entirely different from before. I'd learned more about the truth, love, and strength that define His heart, and I began wanting to emulate that heart. Such a goal requires nothing less than a lifelong commitment to a gradual process. I frequently felt I was going backward, but even so, my desire grew more genuine.

As a manager, I had plenty of opportunities for tough conversations with people—people I reported to, people who reported to me, people in other departments, people in other companies, and with customers—lots and lots of tough conversations. Throughout those years, my appreciation of tough conversations grew as my awareness of the opportunities they offer grew—especially if I approached them with the heart of Jesus in mind.

I wound up having more than my share of tough conversations for two reasons. First, I embraced those that were necessary but that I would have been forgiven for avoiding. Second, I was asked to have tough conversations others believed were important but wanted me to lead. While sometimes they wanted to avoid the situation altogether, my goal was always to empower them to embrace these opportunities the next time.

When I was forty, I started my own training and consulting business for salespeople and managers in the home-building business. The need for tough conversations continued. Some helped salespeople and managers become more successful; others helped them handle their own tough conversations. However, my conversations with them rarely sounded tough in the sense of shouting, criticizing, or arguing; quite the opposite. I was trying to "speak the truth in love" (Ephesians 4:15).

As I became more aware of the value of Jesus' Holy Spirit in tough conversations, my core principles for these encounters became grace, gentleness, compassion, patience, and mutual dignity. I balanced encouragement with accountability and expressing the truth with a loving spirit. As a result, I became stronger.

My joy in tough conversations grew not from the conversations themselves but from the excitement and gratitude for the opportunities they provided. I'm not sure what those opportunities might be, but I've learned they can include

- being an agent of positive transformation,
- accomplishing positive resolution,
- reconciliation, and
- the possible redemption or restoration of another person—perhaps someone I don't like, which can be especially exciting in a surprising way.

These are opportunities Jesus embraced with the joy of showing and sharing God's love. And these are the opportunities He wants us to embrace as well for our own blessing and for blessing others.

Throughout His ministry, Jesus engaged in tough conversations. His love was not always reciprocated or even received. It was frequently rejected, just as it is today. But offering love the way Jesus did (and still does) maximizes the potential of any relationship. It also maximizes the potential of any tough conversation we face.

Truth or Consequences

From the beginning of human civilization, one of our costliest weaknesses has been our fear of engaging in conversations that are difficult but necessary. Whether our fear takes the form of avoidance, anger, aggression, anxiety, intimidation, insult, dishonesty, false encouragement, or giving into something we know is wrong, it's posed a dangerous threat to relationships of all kinds for as long as we've existed.

At times when we *need* to have the conversations we don't *want* to have, we could treasure the opportunities only those moments can provide. But instead, we tend to fear those moments. Our fear causes one of two outcomes: we avoid these conversations, or we mishandle them. On the surface, the fear of mishandling them might sound like a good reason to avoid them, so that's what we do. We decide that avoiding a tough conversation is best because we won't cause any harm. But the problem continues to grow. So the conversation *is* the solution after all, and it's a solution that can provide a wealth of unexpected blessings.

So many relationships—so many lives—are diminished because we bypass the opportunity to speak the truth in love—to say what needs to be said when it needs to be said. We can share so many blessings and achieve so many breakthroughs for us and for others if we're willing to tell the truth when we must in a spirit of selfless love.

Tough conversations are frequently the turning point in relationships. Sometimes, they're turning points in our lives. Occasionally, they're turning points in history. We gain the best outcome from tough conversations when we approach them with a strong heart.

A Strong Heart for Tough Conversations

Jesus showed us the strongest heart of anyone who ever lived; He showed us what the heart of God looks like in human form. What He showed us and taught us applies beautifully to creating a strong heart for tough conversations. He showed us how to use the greatest strength of all—the strength of God's heart—to achieve the most satisfying and productive outcomes from the challenging encounters we face whether with loved ones, strangers, or even enemies.

Tough conversations can have far-reaching effects, and the topic of tough conversations can have far-reaching implications. How we approach tough conversations—how we think about them, feel about them, and engage in them—has much to do with who we want to be. Deciding who we want to be in a tough conversation can inspire us to decide who we want to be in life.

The purpose of this book is to help you get the most out of tough conversations by embracing those moments as opportunities for beautiful transformation for yourself as well as others. We'll explore the skills and mind-set for success in tough conversations in the light of the heart of Jesus—the light in which we find the right kind of strength and influence for achieving the best results.

I'll discuss many examples—some from the Bible, some hypothetical, and some from the learning experiences of my successes and failures. All the stories that include me are true, but the names are fictional. The other stories not from the Bible are illustrations or composites, again with fictional names. Never in the personal experiences I share will I set myself up as a model; the only model in this book is Jesus.

Whether the tough conversation you face is with a family member, friend, teammate, boss, employee, or coworker, this book will help you apply what Jesus, the Son of God, has taught through His words and actions and through the words of the apostles who learned from Him.

CHAPTER 2

Avoid Avoidance

Jesus Has a Tough Conversation with a Rich Young Man

As Jesus started on His way, a man ran up to Him and fell on his knees before Him. "Good teacher," he asked, "what must I do to inherit eternal life?"

"Why do you call me good?" Jesus answered. "No one is good, except God alone. You know the commandments: 'Do not murder, do not commit adultery, do not steal, do not give false testimony, do not defraud, honor your father and mother.'"

"Teacher," he declared, "all these I have kept since I was a boy."

Jesus looked at him and loved him. "One thing you lack," He said. "Go, sell everything you have and give to the poor, and you will have treasure in heaven. Then come, follow me."

At this the man's face fell. He went away sad, because he had great wealth. (Mark 10:17–22)

Tough conversations don't necessarily include angry confrontations. Sometimes, they require us to tell people— gently, quietly, and lovingly—the truth they need to hear to get where they want or need to go. What can make these conversations tough is that what they *need* to hear is not always what they *want* to hear. This was the situation in the story above.

A virtuous young man went to Jesus with a seemingly open heart to learn what he had to do to inherit eternal life. He sounded as though he would do whatever it took, and he just wanted Jesus to tell him what that was.

Jesus spoke with the young man easily and lovingly. He didn't use a tough tone. What made the conversation difficult was that Jesus was delivering a difficult message—a message the young man needed to hear but didn't want to hear. But Jesus jumped right in. He didn't try to placate the young man. He didn't try to cajole the man into following Him. He didn't try to persuade him to use his wealth to support His ministry.

Jesus respected the sincerity of the man's question, and He understood the true need that lay beneath the question. The young man was asking Jesus what he needed to do to increase in favor in the eyes of God. He had proven himself to be virtuous with a lifelong track record of righteous behavior. But he was raising the stakes at that point; he wanted to keep getting better. If he had asked, "Am I doing well enough to get by in this life?" the answer could have been easy. But he was pursuing a higher standard, and the truth would hurt.

The approach Jesus took was selfless. It focused on the needs and well-being of the young man. The truthful answer was that the young man's greatest obstacle to achieving a higher level of righteousness was his wealth. (This is not true of every wealthy person. The problem here was not that the young man had wealth but that he *loved* his wealth—see 1 Timothy 6:10.) Jesus knew that to get the young man where he was trying to go, this truth needed to be addressed head-on. Here was how He did it.

- **He didn't pull any punches.**

Jesus used the young man's compliment—"Good teacher"—as an opportunity for instruction. Since the young man was seeking virtue at the highest level, Jesus wanted him to take his use of the word *good* seriously. Even as the Son of God, who embodied God's goodness, Jesus drew the young man's attention to God the Father as the standard for goodness on which he should focus.

- **He drew out the goodness in the young man and showed His appreciation for that goodness.**

Jesus reviewed God's most-familiar commandments for interacting with other people, and the man testified his lifelong commitment to obeying those commandments. This set up the young man's moment of truth. But before Jesus said another word, He did something huge.

- **"Jesus looked at him and loved him" (Mark 10:21).**

A spirit of love is the most important element you can bring to the table for a tough conversation. Jesus showed He had been profoundly moved by the young man's virtue and by the sincerity and initiative of his question. With a loving demeanor, He led the young man into the difficult part of the conversation.

- **He spoke the truth in love.**

And He spoke it directly. No beating around the bush. He didn't say, "I've got good news and bad news." No hesitation or uncertainty. No avoidance. Just the truth the young man needed to hear.

> "One thing you lack," He said. "Go, sell everything you have and give to the poor, and you will have treasure in heaven. Then come, follow me." At this the man's face fell. He went away sad, because he had great wealth. (Mark 10:21–22)

That was a difficult moment for both of them. The young man learned what was required was a greater sacrifice than he had made before—the sacrifice of the wealth he loved. Jesus had to watch the young man walk away sad, but He had given the man the truth he needed. To reach the level of virtue he strove for, the young man needed to grow beyond his former willingness to *obey* and embrace a new willingness to *sacrifice*.

Jesus had said what needed to be said, and He had said it in love, not just with the appearance of love but with a heart of love.

- **Then He stopped talking.**

Sometimes, this can be the hardest part. Jesus had to watch the young man walk away. This result would have felt like a failure for many of us. We would have been tempted to call out, "Wait! Come back!" Perhaps if we just kept the conversation going, we could figure out a way to soften the message. Maybe we could still salvage a "victory." But tough conversations are not about achieving victory for ourselves; they're about speaking the truth in love.

- **His attitude was selfless.**

Jesus wanted the young man to follow Him; He said so. But He didn't try to coerce or manipulate him. He answered the man's question and explained the cost attached to the answer. He gave the man the choice to accept or reject what he had just learned.

Choice is a precious gift God has given us. The young man needed some space to digest what he had just heard. He needed to decide on his own whether he was willing to make the sacrifice required.

What Avoidance Is About

Tough conversations provide opportunities for breakthroughs. It could be a breakthrough for building a relationship or even for repairing one. It could be a breakthrough for you, or someone else, or for all involved in a conversation. When you embrace the opportunity of a tough conversation, you could become an agent or the recipient of transformation.

The very experience of the conversation can draw out love and courage that had previously lay dormant. It can empower you to conquer fears that previously made you feel helpless. Tough conversations can help you achieve resolutions that you'd previously thought were out of reach. They can lead you to successes in your life that you had never imagined possible.

When we avoid tough conversations, we forfeit such breakthroughs. We succeed in avoiding the stress of the conversation, but we also avoid all the good that could have come from it. The price we pay for avoiding the conversation is often higher than the price of engaging in it. In any endeavor in which success takes us to a higher level, avoiding the endeavor means avoiding the success.

We often think of avoidance as simply "not showing up," but avoidance can also occur *during* a conversation if we avoid the *purpose* of the conversation even as we're engaged in it. For example, suppose you're a manager who must address an employee's need to improve to keep his or her job. You can say you'd like to see better results, but if you don't explain the seriousness of the situation, provide direction for how the employee could achieve the required improvement, and gain a commitment from that employee to improve by the required deadline, you're avoiding what needs to be said when it needs to be said.

In the same way, when a manager tries to discourage an employee to such an extent that he or she quits, the opportunities for a breakthrough are denied. Situations like these can provide breakthroughs for managers and employees alike. Employees can have breakthroughs in their performance and confidence that enable them to turn failure into success.

And the same is true for managers. These conversations can turn managers into leaders—the kind of leaders people want to follow.

One of the main reasons we avoid tough conversations is that we're afraid they won't go well. So our default position is that we're better off avoiding such conversations altogether than risking disaster. Naturally, we don't want to engage in conversations that will do more harm than good, but avoiding tough conversations denies the possibility of potential resolutions and breakthroughs. This produces a whole new level of stress, frustration, and mutual disappointment that causes damage of its own.

Avoidance is dangerous when it becomes our natural comfort zone. Once this happens, the reaction of avoidance becomes instinctive and our justification of avoidance becomes automatic. Here are some of the ways we justify it.

- **"It's not that important."**

We sometimes might think a problem isn't big enough to warrant the hassle of a conversation. The cure may wind up being worse than the disease. Sometimes, this conclusion is the correct one. If we want to make the correct decision, we should make it as objectively as we can, and the way to be objective is to take our self-interest (including our comfort zones) out of play. We saw Jesus do this with the rich young man. We should ask ourselves:

- Is there any potential benefit to the conversation?
- Can a necessary truth be revealed?
- Will the conversation provide an opportunity for anyone to be better off than he or she was before?
- Is it a situation that's better set aside, as is sometimes the case with a personal offense, an accident, or a fluke that's unlikely to happen again?

When our answers to those questions reveal an opportunity for positive change, a conversation initiated in the right spirit is probably better than allowing the issue to fester unresolved.

- **"It'll take care of itself."**

Address this thought the same as the last one.

- **"I don't have the time."**

It's not unusual for us to be "too busy" to do things outside our comfort zones. We always find time for what we believe is most important. If the well-being of another person is at stake, the conversation should move up on the priority list.

- **"I don't want to hurt their feelings."**

Initiating a conversation in a spirit of genuine concern for the well-being of another person reduces the chances of hurting his or her feelings. And if you do hurt anyone's feelings, the chances of fixing it increase. You will sometimes hurt others' feelings especially if they choose defensive positions. They may need to experience hurt feelings to end up seeing what they need to see. Just make sure their well-being is your primary focus throughout the conversation.

- **"I'll wait for a better time."**

The best time to speak the truth in love is usually sooner rather than later. Sometimes, waiting is best for everyone. This is another decision that needs to be made objectively, taking your comfort zone out of the equation. For example, if the issue is, "They're not ready to accept what I have to say," that would be a time to examine whether the issue is with your own comfort zone.

Also consider that sometimes people aren't able to accept what they need to hear until they've first rejected it. When we hear a message that pushes us out of our comfort zones, we may need time to reflect on it in a calmer state. After a time of reflection, we may realize we'll have to step outside our comfort zones to make changes in our thinking or our behavior that will take us to a better place. But when we step out of our comfort zone to accomplish new things, our comfort zone expands to reencompass us.

- **"They're not up to it."**

That may be true. But we could be wrong, and with this kind of opportunity, we need to hope we are. The best way to approach this opportunity for a tough conversation is to assume those with whom we're having conversations will rise to the occasion.

- **"They don't deserve it."**

We cannot decide who deserves to hear the truth that may bring them a breakthrough. We should approach the opportunity we've been given with only their best interests in mind.

- **"It won't do any good."**

This is sometimes true, but it's not a call we can make until after we've tried. I've had many wonderful surprises at times I hadn't expected them. After a while, I realized I should always give it my best shot in a spirit of hope.

- **"I don't have a silver tongue."**

You don't need a silver tongue if you have a golden heart. While it always helps to keep learning better techniques, don't let your lack of confidence deprive others of what you have that could lead them to the resolution or breakthrough they need.

- **"What right do I have?"**

It's about their well-being, not yours, so try to keep the first-person pronouns to a minimum when deciding whether to have a tough conversation. You don't have to be perfect to help someone. If you have concerns about your own credibility in conversations (even to the point of being called a hypocrite), you can admit this to the person and say you still would like to help if you can.

When faced with comfort-zone issues concerning tough conversations, don't ask yourself, *Will this work?* Instead, ask, *What will it take for this to work?* The goal with your comfort zone is always to expand it.

We "avoid avoidance" by realizing the extraordinary blessings a sincere heart can provide during a difficult conversation to you and to others in the conversation. Plus, consider the potential ripple effect of blessings for countless others in the future who might benefit indirectly from your breakthroughs in today's tough conversation.

Let's look more closely at the main reason people avoid tough conversations—fear. We'll spend some time on this. One of the exciting benefits of overcoming the fear of tough conversations is that it involves principles that empower us to overcome many other kinds of fear as well. And everything we need to conquer fear (and its first cousin, anxiety) can be seen in the heart of Jesus.

Jesus Shows Us How to Conquer Fear

Before we talk about strategies for conquering the fear of tough conversations, let's look at the spiritual side of fear. I'm going to take a brief detour from the topic of tough conversations to discuss a few ideas about fear— and how to overcome it—that come from the Word of God, the Bible. I'll bring this teaching back to the heart of this book's message—how to engage in tough conversations with the heart of Jesus.

For me, the most encouraging truth for facing tough conversations is that God has already wired each of us to be good at it if we want to be. He did this by creating us in His own image (Genesis 1:27). He explains what this means throughout His Word, and He sent His Son to show us what God's image looked like in human form so we could emulate it. He is a loving God, and He took human form as a loving man.

When I say God created us in His image, that doesn't mean we think or act like Jesus every moment; He also gave us choice. We can accept who Jesus was or we can reject it. We can accept or reject what He said. We can try to model ourselves after Jesus or choose not to. We can decide how important Jesus is to us. God wired us to be stronger, more satisfied, and more fulfilled when we seek to emulate Jesus. Jesus shows us how living for God works in the human world. But as with wiring in a home, we can choose to use our spiritual wiring or not. And our wiring can get damaged.

The two paragraphs above provide a very short version of a very important concept. I will talk more about God's wiring and how it relates to tough conversations throughout this book.

Love and Fear

Many people from a variety of religious faiths accept the idea that humans experience two primary emotions— love and fear—and that all other emotions grow from these.

God wants our dominant emotion to be love. Therefore, His Enemy, Satan, wants our dominant emotion to be fear.

By creating us in His image, God has wired us for love—His love—the love He showed us in the person of Jesus. God wired each of us the same way He wired Jesus. He sent Jesus to demonstrate our innate wiring and to teach us how to use it most effectively. Jesus showed us how to live as people created in God's image. But God didn't create us as identical robots; He created us as unique individuals with the gift of choice. And one of the choices He gives us is how much of our lives we'll give back to Him—how much we want to live for Him. The more we want to live for Him, the more aware we are of His Spirit in us and the more powerfully we feel His love. The more powerfully we feel His love, the more powerfully we can share that love with others.

The way we experience God's love for us affects the way we feel love for others. We can love others and do so genuinely and deeply for our entire lives without ever thinking about God's love for us. But feeling the miracle of God's love for us adds a dimension to the love we feel for others. The dimension it adds is the love of Jesus—the love He felt for others and the love He feels for us today.

Only One Fear

The only thing God wants us to fear is Him. But that's a good fear—a fear based on reverence instead of insecurity. It isn't a fear of turning toward Him but of turning away from Him. It's not the kind of fear that produces anxiety; it's the kind of fear that produces peace.

God equips those who love Him to overcome fear and anxiety. He didn't wait until the ministry of Jesus to provide this gift. He has always given this special grace for handling fear and anxiety to those who love Him enough to put Him first in their lives. Two of the men who wrote most famously about the blessings of fearing and trusting God were King David and his son, King Solomon, who lived about a thousand years before Jesus. Here are a few verses that David wrote in his Psalms.

The fear of the Lord is pure, enduring forever. (Psalm 19:9)

The Lord is the stronghold of my life—of whom shall I be afraid? (Psalm 27:1)

I sought the Lord and He answered me; he delivered me from all my fears. (Psalm 34:4)

The angel of the Lord encamps around those who fear Him, and He delivers them. (Psalm 34:7)

Solomon's Proverbs included the following.

The fear of the Lord is the beginning of wisdom. (Proverbs 9:10)

To fear the Lord is to hate evil. (Proverbs 8:13)

A wise man fears the Lord and shuns evil. (Proverbs 14:16)

He who fears the Lord has a secure fortress.
(Proverbs 14:26)

Through the fear of the Lord a man avoids
evil. (Proverbs 16:6)

Solomon had an emphatic conclusion to his search for
life's meaning in his book of Ecclesiastes:

Fear God and keep His commandments, for
this is the whole duty of man. (Ecclesiastes
12:13)

Jesus wasn't introducing a new concept in turning
to God to overcome fear and anxiety; He was living it in
the context of love. He showed how love—for God and for
one another—provides courage and strength for dealing
with fear in all situations. It's an example that applies
beautifully to those times when we need to engage in
tough conversations. But first, let's dig a little deeper into
what Jesus and a few of His followers said about fear in
general, and we'll see how He applied it directly to the
kinds of conversations we may be inclined to avoid.

Love Conquers Fear

Jesus modeled the truth that love conquers fear in
the hearts of those who live for God. It isn't that we don't
experience fear or anxiety when we live for God; Christ's
love empowers us to conquer our fear and anxiety with
love. Jesus' apostle John, known as the apostle of love,

wrote, "There is no fear in love. But perfect love drives out fear" (1 John 4:18).

What this means for tough conversations is that a spirit of love provides the strength we need to embrace tough conversations without fear or anxiety. The next chapter will explain exactly how this works, but my point here is that again and again throughout His ministry, Jesus faced harrowing adversity from enemies who put their self-interests above their love for God. Each time, His love for His Father and for all people gave Him courage and purpose in the face of fear. His love continued to triumph even as He hung on the cross at the hands of His enemies. He personified the truth that "there is no fear in love" and that "perfect love"—selfless, godly love—"drives out fear" (1 John 4:18).

"Do Not Worry"

Jesus wants our love for God to conquer worry and anxiety as well as fear. A life free of worry and fear is what God wants for us. He created us with the capacity to experience that magnificent existence when we put Him first. This doesn't mean our lives will be free of adversity but that our spirit will be free from worry and fear in times of adversity if we commit our lives to Him in a spirit of love—gratefully receiving His love for us and extending that love to others because they are also His creation. These principles also become the "rules of engagement" for tough conversations. Here's how Jesus told us not to worry.

> Do not worry about your life ... Who of you by worrying can add a single hour to his life? ... Seek first God's kingdom and His righteousness, and all these things [you need] will be given to you as well. Therefore do not worry about tomorrow, for tomorrow will worry about itself. Each day has enough trouble of its own. (Matthew 6:25–34)

His apostle Paul added,

> Do not be anxious about anything, but in everything, by prayer and petition, with thanksgiving, present your requests to God. And the peace of God, which transcends all understanding, will guard your hearts and minds in Christ Jesus. (Philippians 4:6–7)

Jesus explained the gentleness of His love—God's love—like this.

> Come to me, all you who are weary and burdened, and I will give you rest. Take my yoke upon you and learn from me, for I am gentle and humble in heart, and you will find rest for your souls. (Matthew 11:28–29)

These three passages explain the spirit God wants to abide in us. This spirit is especially important for achieving the best possible resolution in difficult encounters.

We've taken a brief detour into God's general instructions for conquering fear to set the stage for embracing instead of avoiding tough conversations. Let's zero in on some ideas that are more specific to these encounters.

What Is the Fear of Tough Conversations Really About?

In my work over the years as a salesperson, manager, and consultant assisting other people through their difficult encounters, I learned that the biggest obstacle in tough conversations was fear, and the most frequent result of this fear was avoidance. In cases in which the conversation wasn't avoided, the biggest obstacle to satisfactory outcomes was also fear. In many cases, the fear was shared by both people involved, so fear became the dominant mood of the entire conversation. What's that fear about? It's usually about two things: fear of "What will become of me?" and "fear of man."

The first fear is overcome by disengaging from concern about your own well-being in the conversation and focusing instead on the well-being of the other person. When you focus on maintaining the well-being of the other person, your own well-being takes care of itself. Say to yourself, *I'll get through this conversation just fine. I need to make sure the other person gets through it fine too.*

We're wired as creatures made in God's image—the image personified by Jesus—so we're always at our best and strongest when we're focused on the well-being of people other than ourselves, and we're always at our worst and weakest when we focus on our own well-being. This doesn't mean we're less "successful" by worldly standards (at least in the short term) when we focus on ourselves; it means that focusing on others makes us emotionally stronger because it's a higher spiritual state. I will explain this in more detail in the next chapter.

The second fear—fear of man—is introduced by Solomon in Proverbs 29:25: "Fear of man will prove to be a snare, but whoever trusts in the Lord is kept safe." Fear of man doesn't refer to the fear we feel when looking down the barrel of a gun but to the fear of what other people will think. Jesus taught that when we focus on pleasing God more than on pleasing men, we perform at our highest level in a more peaceful, powerful state. God created us to be stronger when we turn to Him so we *would* turn to Him.

Saying that we are "kept safe" refers to safety from fear—spiritual safety—not necessarily from physical danger. Fearing God in the righteous, loving, trusting way Jesus did provides us with emotional strength to enter tough conversations without fear.

Let's look at how Jesus lived out what we've been discussing in His own approach to tough conversations.

How Jesus Approached Tough Conversations

Jesus' ministry required Him to tell people many things they didn't want to hear. If His greatest desire had been merely popularity for His own sake, His true ministry would never have gotten off the ground. His ministry was never about telling people what they wanted to hear but telling them what they needed to hear. He put their well-being above His own and spoke the truth in love.

He sometimes addressed their need to understand the path they were on so they could choose different paths. Other times, He led them where they were trying to go, knowing they needed encouragement that the effort was truly worth it. He never avoided tough conversations that served the well-being of another, and He never procrastinated in telling the truth; He told it as soon as the opportunity arose.

Even when He rebuked others, His desire was for their redemption. They deserved to know what they needed to know even if it wasn't what they wanted to hear. The tough conversations gave them the opportunity to choose a path that would lead to their redemption. Then at least they could make their choice of how to respond based on the truth.

He spoke the truth in love, but He never sugarcoated it, and He was never stopped by the fear that harm might come to Him. He put the well-being of others above His own. His apostle Paul captured this spirit.

> Do nothing out of selfish ambition or vain conceit, but in humility consider others better than yourselves. Each of you should look not only to your own interests, but also to the interests of others. (Philippians 2:3–4)

This is how we become emotionally strong and how we "avoid avoidance" when the need arises for a difficult encounter.

We've already seen the spirit and technique Jesus used when he spoke the truth in love to the rich young man. He had the option of gaining a wealthy new follower just by telling him he was already good enough. Jesus had no desire to criticize the man, tear him down, or lift Himself up as superior. The man came to Him to ask how he could improve even though he was already a righteous man. Asking how we can improve often results in an answer we don't want to hear. It's a virtuous question that can initiate a demanding discussion. It's a crucial question that requires both parties to be sincere. The encounter left the man crestfallen but enriched. He had learned how to attain his goal of higher virtue. It was not an easy decision to make, and he couldn't make it on the spot. He could only walk away sad. We aren't told of his final decision, but that wasn't the point of the story. The point is that we must all deal with this crucial decision on our own, but we need to be open to the tough conversations through which we can teach and learn, speaking the truth in love.

Let's look at a few other situations in which Jesus embraced tough conversations.

Jesus and the Adulteress

The teachers of the law and the Pharisees brought in a woman caught in adultery. They made her stand before the group and said to Jesus, "Teacher, this woman was caught in the act of adultery. In the Law Moses commanded us to stone such women. Now what do you say?" They were using this question as a trap, in order to have a basis for accusing Him ... When they kept on questioning Him, He straightened up and said to them, "If any one of you is without sin, let him be the first to throw a stone at her." ... At this, those who heard began to go away one at a time, until only Jesus was left, with the woman still standing there. Jesus straightened up and asked her, "Woman, where are they? Has no one condemned you?"

"No one, sir," she said.

"Then neither do I condemn you," Jesus declared. "Go now and leave your life of sin." (John 8:3–11)

As soon as the teachers and Pharisees asked their question, Jesus knew He was under threat. Any answer He gave would put Him at risk. The woman was guilty of the charge against her. Under the Law, they had a right to stone her, but that wasn't the question they had asked. They had asked, "What do you say?" They wanted to know His opinion of the situation—whether He believed what they were about to do was right.

Were they sincere about learning the truth, or did they only want to get Him in trouble? What if His answer got Him killed and they stoned the woman anyway? Could anyone have blamed Him if He had chosen to dodge the question? He was heading into a tough conversation.

He could easily have said, "It's your decision." He could have said, "You're obeying the Law. How can I criticize that?" Or He could have said, "This is your problem. Why are you trying to make it mine?"

Instead, He answered their question at the highest possible level—the level of compassion and forgiveness. He wanted them to understand that while they had the legal option of killing the woman, they also had the option of compassion and forgiveness just as they would be forgiven by a compassionate Father if they asked for it in a spirit of sincere repentance. Jesus wanted each of the teachers and Pharisees to have that option of repentance, and He wanted the woman to have it as well. To Jesus, the Law was always important but not at the expense of a godly heart.

Jesus spoke His answer kindly but truthfully, gently but firmly. He modeled for us the way to speak the truth with love. His answer didn't let anyone off the hook. He addressed the crowd's harshness and the woman's sin; He told them both that they needed to change their ways to live righteously. As with the rich young man, Jesus answered the question that had been asked, and He made sure the woman understood that the correct response to forgiveness was to get off the wrong road and onto the right one.

Jesus Explained the Cost of Following Him

Here we see a very different kind of tough conversation. This time, Jesus was speaking to His followers, telling them what to expect from a life of following Him. By worldly standards, this was the time for a high-energy pep rally. The highlight of this pep rally would be an inspiring vision of an exciting journey toward a destiny of wealth, fame, and comfort for all who stayed with Him.

But He led His team down a different path, and they needed to know what the path would be like. He would tell the truth that needed to be told and speak the truth in love. He would not deal recklessly with the well-being of those who were counting on Him for the truth. There was definitely good news to be shared—great news! There was also a price to pay. So often, leaders avoid the hard message by focusing on the good news and then soft-pedaling the bad news with a comment like, "Obviously, not every day will be all roses. Life never is. But if you hang in there, the payoff will be incredible!" Jesus said it differently.

"The Son of Man must suffer many things and be rejected by the elders, chief priests and teachers of the law, and He must be killed and on the third day raised to life."

Then He said to them all: "If anyone would come after Me, he must deny himself and take up his cross daily and follow Me. For whoever wants to save his life will lose it, but whoever loses His life for Me will save it. What good is it for a man to gain the whole world, and yet lose or forfeit His very self? If any man is ashamed of Me and My words, the Son of Man will be ashamed of him when He comes in His glory and in the glory of the Father and of the holy angels." (Luke 9:22–26)

Notice the way Jesus foretold His death in the same tone that He foretold His resurrection. If He had been focused on "selling" them on following Him (a selfish motivation), He would have explained the good news in a way that overwhelmed the bad news. But He was more concerned about their well-being than His own, so His focus was on selfless truthfulness.

This conversation was not tough in the sense of confrontation but in the sense of putting His self-interest at risk to explain tough standards and set correct expectations for those who were trying to decide whether to put their trust in Him.

Jesus taught many hard things, but He never sugarcoated His message. He was a straight shooter. Yet the purpose of His messages was always the well-being of those to whom He spoke. Rather than cajole or persuade, He left it for them to decide.

Jesus Sends Out the Twelve Apostles

Another difficult message was required when He gave His twelve apostles instructions for their first missionary trip without Him. He didn't say, "If you do what I tell you, everything will go smoothly." Some of His instructions were wonderfully exciting, some encouraging, some were possibly disappointing, and still others potentially frightening. He included them all in this message. Here are a few examples from Matthew 10. Having given them "authority to drive out evil spirits and to heal every sickness and disease" (v. 1), He told them,

> As you go, preach this message: "The kingdom of heaven is near." Heal the sick,

raise the dead, cleanse those who have leprosy, drive out demons. Freely you have received, freely give. (Matthew 10:7–8)

He could have stopped there and concluded with, "When you get back, you'll have a nice fat bonus waiting for you." But instead, He had more instructions.

Do not take along any gold or silver or copper in your belts; take no bag for the journey, or extra tunic, or sandals or a staff; for the worker is worth his keep. Whatever town or village you enter, search for some worthy person there and stay at his house until you leave.

If anyone will not welcome you or listen to your words, shake the dust off your feet when you leave that home or town, (Matthew 10:11, 14)

They had to count on being sustained one day at a time, and success was not always guaranteed. "I am sending you out like sheep among wolves" (Matthew 10:16). Any second thoughts yet? Then how about this?

Be on your guard against men; they will hand you over to the local councils and flog you in their synagogues. On My account you will be brought before governors and kings as witnesses to them and to the Gentiles. But when they arrest you, do not worry

about what to say or how to say it. At that
time you will be given what to say, for it
will not be you speaking, but the Spirit of
your Father speaking through you ... All
men will hate you because of Me, but He
who stands firm to the end will be saved.
When you are persecuted in one place, flee
to another. (Matthew 10:17–23)

In providing instructions with correct expectations,
Jesus included a remarkable mix of terrors and
reassurances—warnings and encouragements. One of
the magnificent elements of the Gospels is the way Jesus
expressed His love for those who committed their lives
to Him. He spoke the truth in love for their sakes, not
for His own. His words were filled with love and truth.
His followers would live a life of glorious miracles and
triumphs, but they would pay a price of suffering along the
way. Yet through it all, He would be with them through
His Holy Spirit—throughout their lives on earth and then
throughout eternity. Then, as always, He gave them the
choice of whether that deal sounded good to them.

We again see Jesus providing direction without
sugarcoating. He knew His followers would face danger
and hardship, and He wanted them to know what they
were getting into. But there would also be blessings beyond
description.

There are two ways to avoid a tough conversation.
One is to avoid it altogether. The other is to engage in the
conversation but avoid saying everything that needs to be
said. Jesus' commitment to the well-being of His followers
blew away any temptation to avoid the conversation or

any important details relevant to it. We will now look at a different kind of tough conversation.

Martha and Mary

In the story of Martha and Mary, Jesus has to deal with a "personnel" complaint. Martha complained that her sister Mary wasn't pulling her weight, leaving Martha to pick up the slack. She complained that it was just not right and that the boss, Jesus, needed to man up and take control of the situation.

Martha's plight was one most of us can sympathize with. Mary was taking advantage of Martha, and it wasn't fair. But often when we complain that something isn't fair, what we mean is that it isn't fair to "me." If we take self-interest out of the equation, we see a bigger picture. It turned out to be Martha, not Mary, with whom Jesus needed to have the tough conversation. He did so unwaveringly, with the gentle confidence that came from godly love. "In perfect love there is no fear."

> As Jesus and His disciples were on their way, He came to a village where a woman named Martha opened her home to Him. She had a sister called Mary, who sat at the Lord's feet listening to what He said. But Martha was distracted by all the preparations that had to be made. She came to Him and asked, "Lord, don't you care that my sister has left me to do all the work by myself? Tell her to help me!" "Martha, Martha," the

Lord answered, "you are worried and upset about many things, but only one thing is needed. Mary has chosen what is better, and it will not be taken away from her." (Luke 10:38–42)

Conversations can seem troublesome, perhaps even troublesome enough to avoid, when we have to tell people we won't give them what they want or we tell them no in a way they view as insulting and we wind up regretting what we said.

Jesus felt sincere compassion for Martha. Even saying her name twice conveyed endearment. Each sister was being attentive to Jesus in her own way. Martha's connection was with her work, while Mary's connection was with Jesus. Martha's sense of responsibility was commendable, but it left her miserable. Jesus wanted Martha to share in Mary's joy of human connection—a blessing that could not be taken away. He refused to give Martha what she wanted, but He gave her what He knew she needed. He didn't want Martha to criticize Mary for giving the gift of heartfelt attention. How many relationships suffer because people believe it's more important to work than to enjoy each other's company? Jesus wanted Martha to enjoy the fuller life that came from richer relationships. He cared enough about her to risk an uncomfortable moment to give her a more comfortable life.

It might have been easier to placate Martha with expressions of appreciation. "Martha, I really appreciate all the work you do. You're absolutely right. Mary should carry her share of the load. As soon as there's an opportunity, I'll ask her to give you a hand." Or He could have said, "Let's not make a scene about it. Next time, it will be Mary's turn, and I'll let you sit at my feet." But Jesus took the tougher route—a gentle, loving rebuke that showed Martha a path to a happier life with more peace of mind. Sadly, these are the conversations we often choose to avoid.

Jesus mastered a tough conversation because He put Martha's well-being ahead of His own comfort. There's a bonus: when we're that committed to using tough conversations to bless others, it takes discomfort out of play. The discomfort of a tough conversation is replaced by the joy of improving the life of another even when that blessing is not immediately received by the other.

In the case of Martha and Mary, it was all among friends, as it was with the conversations He had with His apostles. But sometimes, His tough conversations were with serious adversaries, including people who wanted Him killed.

Jesus Confronts the Pharisees

One of the most dangerous threats to Jesus' ministry was the hypocrisy of the Pharisees. The Pharisees made up a Jewish sect that wielded a lot of influence in the Jewish faith. Some of their leaders were driven by self-serving rather than compassionate motivations. They didn't teach about God's love or about loving one another in a godly spirit; they professed a godliness they didn't live.

God's desire for humans, whom He created in His image, has always been to draw us closer to Him so we can experience His love more fully. As we experience God's love more fully, we desire to share that love with others. Jesus sought to draw people closer to God so they would love Him more deeply, experience His love for them more fully, and love one another more selflessly. When Jesus was asked which of God's commandments was most important, this was His answer.

> "Love the Lord your God with all your heart and with all your soul and with all your mind." This is the first and greatest commandment. And the second is like it: "Love your neighbor as yourself." All the Law and the Prophets hang on these two commandments. (Matthew 22:38–40)

The Pharisees knew these commandments, which were written in the Law they professed to live by, but they didn't live by them. Ignoring these priorities God had taught through Moses took them farther from God instead of closer to Him. The influence of their leadership took many other Jews farther from God as well. So this was an extremely serious matter Jesus needed to confront. This confrontation was a major reason that the Pharisees considered Jesus a dangerous enemy of the Jewish religion.

The critical differences between their beliefs required Jesus to have many difficult discussions with the Pharisees. In many cases, He knew such conversations would put His life at risk.

Once again, He was giving information His listeners needed. The well-being of the Pharisees was important to Him. On the occasions when Pharisees came to Him in an earnest search for truth, His tone was patient and gentle. But the tone of His approach needed to change when He was dealing with those whose primary aim was to destroy Him. His love was still there, and His desire for their redemption, well-being, and reconciliation with God was genuine, but He had to be aggressive in His tone to demonstrate this was no game, no simple debate, or recreational verbal sparring. The stakes were high. It was about preventing an entire religion from turning against God. He had to show He wouldn't waver or negotiate. He had to call out the Pharisees publicly and decisively for the destruction they were causing.

One example of such a conversation occurred in Luke 11:37–54, a long passage worth reading in its entirety. For our purposes here, we'll look at a few verses that demonstrate how Jesus approached a very difficult situation in circumstances far different from the earlier examples we've seen. The specific issue in these verses concerns the right balance between traditional ceremony, which the Pharisees emphasized, and a godly heart, which the Pharisees ignored.

> Woe to you Pharisees, because you give God a tenth of your mint, rue and all other kinds of garden herbs, but you neglect justice and the love of God. You should have practiced the latter without leaving the former undone. (Luke 11:42)

> Woe to you Pharisees, because you love the most important seats in the synagogues and greetings in the marketplaces. (Luke 11:43)

One of the experts in the law answered Him, "Teacher, when you say these things, you insult us also." Jesus replied, "And you experts in the law, woe to you, because you load people down with burdens they can hardly carry, and you yourselves will not lift one finger to help them." (Luke 11:45–46)

Woe to you experts in the law, because you have taken away the key to knowledge. You yourselves have not entered, and you have hindered those who were entering. (Luke 11:53)

When Jesus left there, the Pharisees and the teachers of the law began to oppose Him fiercely and to besiege Him with questions, waiting to catch Him in something He might say. (Luke 11:53–54)

Since the Pharisees ultimately achieved their goal of having Jesus killed, was Jesus' approach to this tough conversation the correct one?

The approach Jesus used was not focused on His self-interest but on the well-being of others, including even the Pharisees. He was bringing godliness into its proper focus. His motivation was not to harm His enemies but to provide a path for their redemption and reconciliation with God. His anger was righteous, not venomous. He was rebuking the sins of selfishness and pride and trying to prevent those sins from luring others down the same path. He addressed specific behaviors that showed their need to redirect their hearts toward God and toward a godly love of others. He pointed them toward a higher form of leadership.

Jesus taught us that we cannot always expect immediate gratification from doing what we know is right and that we cannot anticipate all the future good a righteous encounter can produce. We engage in the conversation fearlessly because it's what others need to hear. The conversation in the verses above has improved the lives of many people over the past two thousand years by redirecting their focus from their own well-being to a selfless commitment to the well-being of others.

Many people have developed closer relationships with a loving God because they realized godly love must not be compromised by self-serving motives. Embracing the tough conversations that need to occur will often have wonderful, important results far beyond what we can imagine even when they don't appear to benefit us. It's one way we live life to the fullest.

A Personal Application

One of my clients employed a manager whose desire to advance his career endangered the careers of others. I'll call him Roger. Roger's ambition had escalated into slander and threats. On one occasion, he concluded a threat by saying, "If you repeat this to anyone, I'll deny it, and I'll deny it to your face." Since no one stopped him, his attitude became more arrogant and his behavior more menacing.

Everyone who worked for him wanted him stopped, but some feared his retaliation. They asked me to intervene and gave me their permission to tell Roger what I knew. I told Roger that he was causing a lot of harm but that with the right approach, he could still regain the respect of his team. This was the truth. The team had told me they would support him if he sincerely wanted to become a good manager. Roger told me to mind my own business. Who did I think I was? What right did I have to tell him how to do his job?

I told him I wouldn't stand by and watch him hurt salespeople and the other sales manager, his counterpart, with lies and intimidation. I told him that I sincerely believed he could be a fine manager and that the only thing stopping him was his own fear of failure, which he had no reason to fear. He asked what I meant when I said I wouldn't just stand by. I told him I'd go to upper management. He told me that he would deny it and that they would believe him over me. Then he upped the ante by assuring me he could hurt me more than I could hurt him.

I had committed myself to engaging in this tough conversation in the spirit I have described, but I failed to get the result I had hoped for.

I went to upper management and told them what I knew. They confronted Roger, who, true to his word, denied it. Upper management called a meeting of the employees, who confirmed what I had told them. The employees told me about the meeting, so I went back and told upper management that I knew. They told me they would pursue the matter. My weeklong visit ended, and I was due back again two months later.

When I returned, I was surprised to learn that upper management had never talked with Roger again about the problem. Roger avoided me during the entire trip. Upper management had avoided the conversation with Roger. There was plenty of avoidance to go around. The tough conversation that was the only way to fix the problem never happened, and it never would.

Upper management told me the problem had blown over, which the employees told me was not true. I told upper management I could no longer support an organization that said Roger's treatment of his employees was acceptable. They said that they were sorry to see me go.

I was profoundly disappointed that my approach hadn't worked. I sincerely believed I'd handled the situation with the heart of Jesus, and I felt His example had been tremendously valuable, but evil had prevailed. I also believed if I stayed around, my acceptance of the avoidance would make matters only worse. I believed I had faced the problem head-on; I had not avoided it. I didn't believe there was an option to "keep on fighting" in this case, and I didn't feel I was running away. This was my biggest client, so I didn't feel the choice I had made was selfish. I was gone. It made me extremely sad because I had grown very fond of the people I had worked with there, including the upper managers. I felt they were really good people. All they did wrong was avoid one tough conversation.

Five months later, I got a call from the president. "Rich, I wanted to let you know Roger's gone. I want to apologize it took so long. It's a heck of a thing when an outsider has to be the conscience of a company. But thank you for being that conscience. I'm calling to ask if you'll come back."

So often, we avoid tough conversations because we don't feel strong in the situation. We feel we need a greater position of strength to engage in the conversation effectively. But where does our position of strength for a tough conversation come from? The next chapter will answer that.

CHAPTER 3

Tough Conversations from a Position of Strength

The best way to gain a position of strength in a tough conversation is to focus on the needs, well-being, and dignity of the adversary. (For my purposes in this chapter, I will use the term "adversary" to refer to the person[s] with whom you're having the conversation even though you may enjoy a friendly or loving relationship with them and even though the conversation may not include any conflict or animosity. Sometimes, the "adversity" is merely a feeling of awkwardness, but the feeling is strong enough to cause anxiety.)

In the ways of the world, focusing on the needs, dignity, and well-being of an adversary may sound counterintuitive, but it makes perfect sense if you consider the way love and fear each influence a tough conversation. Remember what John, the apostle of love, wrote about love and fear: "There is no fear in love, but perfect love drives out fear" (1 John 4:18). Here's where we bring that verse to life in creating a position of strength for tough conversations.

The Vulnerability of Fear

Fear is our greatest vulnerability in tough conversations. Of the two primary emotions, fear is the one that creates our position of weakness in tough conversations. The other primary emotion—love—creates our position of strength. We might feel anxious about engaging in a conversation for a variety of reasons, but most of them are rooted in fear. Here are a few:

- fear that the adversary will make us look or feel bad
- fear that we will make ourselves look or feel bad
- fear that we will make the adversary look or feel bad
- fear that we will "lose"
- fear that we will get soft and give in
- fear that no good will come from the conversation, only harm—to us, the adversary, or both
- fear that the conversation will get ugly
- fear that the conversation will damage or destroy the relationship

Some of these fears may appear more selfish than others. But directly or indirectly, they all trace back to the fear something bad will happen to us even if what happens to us is the guilt of hurting someone else.

When I say fear creates our position of weakness and vulnerability in tough conversations, I'm not saying this fear is evil. I want only to prevent it from undermining a necessary conversation. If a conversation needs to occur, we need a way to neutralize our fear so it cannot inject harm into the conversation or prevent it from occurring.

Fear is a normal *initial* emotion to experience when we anticipate certain conversations. For example, if you have to tell a valuable employee he or she is being laid off and you know the negative consequences to him or her and the family involved, the anxiety of initiating the conversation is connected with sympathy.

Your anxiety might come from sympathy as well as guilt if you have to tell a neighbor you've just killed her pet with your car. You'd experience a frightening anxiety rooted in sympathetic grief if you had to tell a friend his wife had been killed in an accident. You want to avoid any of these conversations in the sense of wishing the tragedy were not real. Your fear of the conversation would need to be managed for the good of the other person as well as yourself. You know you've got to give the best of yourself to them. How is this kind of fear managed? It's managed through love—love in the form of compassion.

The same truth applies to firing someone who's been a terrible employee but will continue to live comfortably off an inheritance. Whatever anxiety may exist that could cause fear of the conversation (even if it's the fear of a possible retaliation), you still need to get the employee through the conversation with his dignity intact. This doesn't mean telling him he was a better employee than he was or that you like him any more than you do. It just means remembering God created him and loves him and behaving toward him with that perspective. That is a legitimate form of compassion. It's also a valuable position of strength in the conversation.

A position of strength in a tough conversation is far deeper than a mere tactical maneuver. It includes courage, fortitude, and steadfastness. Whether the conversation is about one of the topics just mentioned, or telling someone to treat you differently, or telling an employee she needs to improve her behavior or performance, or telling a menacing neighbor you'll have him arrested the next time he sets foot on your property, you have decided the conversation is necessary. You must figure out how to manage whatever fear or anxiety might derail the conversation before its purpose is fulfilled. Once you commit yourself to the conversation, you commit to neutralizing your fear so that

- you engage in the conversation instead of avoiding it,
- you engage in the conversation in a way that gains the best possible result for everyone, and
- you move the conversation along to completion, not letting it be aborted.

A Tough Conversation Is Ministry

If you think of tough conversations as a ministry, you start down the road to a position of strength—the best kind of strength. Not strength in the sense of conquest, but in the sense of resolution—the best resolution. Not with the purpose of defending yourself, but with the purpose of honoring the needs, dignity, and well-being of your adversary. When you approach tough conversations as ministry, you'll find your position of strength more easily.

Let's talk about needs first. Focusing on the needs of your adversary enables you to focus on that adversary as a human being while still focusing on the issue. When I talk about honoring (or ministering to) the needs of your adversaries, I don't mean indulging their desires or whims. I'm talking about honoring their *true* needs, and that honoring begins with sincerely wanting to understand those needs. This principle applies to loved ones or enemies. In either case, understanding and honoring their needs is your position of strength.

Focusing on the needs of the adversary will get the conversation where it needs to go. That may be different from getting you where you want to go or getting your adversary where he or she wants to go. But if you can get the conversation where *it* needs to go, you'll maximize your opportunity.

You're not ignoring your own needs by focusing solely on the needs of the adversary because your needs are already internalized. You now want to internalize the adversary's needs beside yours. As Paul said, "Each of you should look not only to your own needs, but also to the interests of others" (Philippians 2:4).

Dignity

Focusing on their needs means focusing not only on what they tell you they need but also on what they need to gain from the conversation simply because they are human. One of the greatest needs every human being has is dignity. Our dignity is perhaps our most valuable worldly possession. It includes being treated with respect and also being taken seriously. One of our greatest sources of emotional misery is the belief we're not being taken seriously. Being taken seriously is a mark of our dignity.

Some people behave as though they've given up on their own dignity, so they don't treat others with dignity either.

That's what happened to Andy, the fellow at boarding school. He didn't seem to value his own dignity, so he behaved as though he didn't value others' dignity. But even though he seemed to have given up on dignity, he never stopped wanting it. In creating us in His image, God created us to want dignity and to respond to it. Dignity is a gift for which everyone is grateful. Being treated with dignity rejuvenated Andy, and he became eager to give it to others. That is what we need to do in tough conversations.

Selflessness

I began this chapter with, "The best way to gain a position of strength in a tough conversation is to focus on the needs, dignity, and well-being of the adversary." If that's the best way to gain a position of strength, what exactly is the position of strength we're trying to gain? The greatest position of strength we can have in a tough conversation is selflessness. That's the way we were wired. We were created in God's image, so we function at our highest level of strength, performance, and effectiveness when we emulate Jesus.

I emphasize that when I talk about how God has wired us, I'm not saying we're wired so that we *have* to emulate Jesus; I'm saying that we are stronger, more effective, and more satisfied when we *do* emulate Jesus. In any endeavor that involves other people (not just tough conversations), we're created so that the strongest position we can take is to focus on this question, "What are the needs of the other people involved?" A position of strength doesn't come from,

"What's best for me?" or "What do I feel like doing?" That's where our position of weakness comes from. Just as we're wired so that selflessness is our position of strength, we're wired so that selfishness is our position of weakness.

We're designed to be at our best and strongest when we focus on the well-being of others, and we're designed to be at our worst and weakest when we focus on our well-being. With all due respect to Darwinism and our "survival instinct," we as a species have not continued to progress because we do a better job than any other species of taking care of ourselves. We continue to progress because we do a better job of taking care of each other. We're more aware of the need to take care of the rest of our species— beyond ourselves and our immediate family—than any other creature.

Let's take the verse I quoted from Paul a moment ago and combine it with the verse that comes before it.

> Do nothing out of selfish ambition or vain conceit, but in humility consider others better than yourselves. Each of you should look not only to your own interests, but to the interests of others. (Philippians 2:3–4)

This is the attitude with which Jesus washed the feet of His apostles at the Last Supper. He did this knowing He would give up His life the next day. He would die for an unusual purpose—so sinners would gain the opportunity to be restored to an intimate relationship with the God who created them in a spirit of love. And Jesus had the greatest position of strength—even in His crucifixion—of any person who ever lived.

Richard Tiller

The Power of Selflessness in
Tough Conversations

The tough conversations Jesus had—with those who loved Him and with those who hated Him—transformed the world. Tough conversations provide the opportunity for transformation whether or not that opportunity is embraced.

We feel stronger in a tough conversation when we say to ourselves, *I don't need to worry about myself in this conversation. I'll be fine. My dignity is intact. If I focus on the needs of the adversary, my needs will be met. If I focus on his dignity, my own will increase. If I focus on his well-being, mine will take care of itself.* This is extremely powerful thinking! It's a mighty position of strength for a tough conversation.

One of the worst ways to diminish the dignity of adversaries is to cause them to feel you don't take them seriously. A remarkable quality of Jesus' interactions was the way He took people seriously who were not taken seriously by others. He admonished them, He told them to shape up, He confronted them head-on, and He sometimes belittled their hypocrisy. But He never stripped them of their dignity. He was criticized for honoring the dignity of those who were marginalized by everyone else—the sick, the foreign, the sinful. He sought their redemption. That's why He has had more followers than anyone else. When you have more followers than anyone else in history and more followers today than during your mortal lifetime two thousand years ago, that's a position of strength.

Strength for the Adversary?

How do my adversaries fit into all this? If I want a position of strength in tough conversations, don't I want my adversaries to have a position of weakness? And if I'm trying to eliminate my own fear, shouldn't I try to increase my adversaries' fear?

No, quite the opposite. Just as I want to advocate my adversaries' dignity, I also want to advocate their encouragement. And that's not encouragement to do wrong, but righteous encouragement—the kind of encouragement that nurtures their dignity. Encouragement in wrongdoing doesn't nurture dignity, it undermines it. Paul wrote, "Encourage one another and build each other up" (1 Thessalonians 5:11).

Providing the right encouragement for my adversary creates a huge position of strength for me. Jesus encouraged people in the sense of wanting to help them improve their lives. He showed that there is always hope for improving our lives no matter how hopeless our situation may seem.

Just as I don't want to experience fear in tough conversations, I don't want my adversaries to experience it either. The only thing I want to fear is God, and if I'm trying to encourage my adversaries, the only fear I want them to experience is the fear of God as well. That's the kind of fear Jesus sought to instill in His friends and enemies alike.

We can try to use intimidation as a tactic for controlling a tough conversation, and it may even appear to be a successful tactic for a while. Ultimately though, intimidation poses more risk to the intimidator than to the victim, and this can often be in ways we cannot comprehend in the moment. A tough conversation is most successful when there's no fear on either side. It's simply unproductive to try to instill fear in an adversary. It's more productive if we use our own position of strength to help create strength in the heart of our adversary as well. The best result is achieved when the position of strength is shared by the opponents through mutual respect, mutual accountability, mutual encouragement, and mutual dignity. The adversary is blessed by the conversation as much as we are. Everyone comes out of it better off than he or she went into it. That's the ideal. But sometimes, that ideal is beyond our reach because our adversary is not pursuing the same ideal.

For our part, we can seek a position of strength by focusing on the needs, well-being, and dignity of the adversary. By approaching the encounter selflessly. By keeping compassion in the equation and fear out of it as best we can. But we never have to kowtow; we never have to grovel. There's no weakness in any of the principles we're discussing here—only strength. It all relates to how we've been wired by God in His image—described in His Word and lived by His Son.

But what if both parties don't follow these principles? What if the adversaries we face believe the opposite of everything discussed here? What if their only desire in the confrontation is victory and their only concern is for themselves? All the principles still apply to your position; your position of strength is still the same. You simply may not enjoy the satisfaction of a transformational experience. I remember a tough conversation I was in that lasted four and a half hours, and it had no transformational effect whatsoever as far as I know. It was a total nuisance. Yet it still increased my desire to embrace the opportunities that might lie in tough conversations in the future. Here's what happened.

High Noon

When I was vice president of sales for a home builder, a construction superintendent called me one morning to tell me about a disastrous presettlement inspection the day before. The inspection was supposed to last between one and two hours. The superintendent told me that the customer (I'll call him Dan) had berated him for eleven hours nonstop the day before. I asked the superintendent how Dan's wife liked the home, and he said she'd mostly stayed quiet.

The whole thing was a shakedown—Dan just wanted money. His profession was negotiating, and he actually called himself a "master negotiator who always got what he wanted." Saying that about himself seemed like an odd strategy to me. Nevertheless, Dan was relentlessly abusive to the superintendent. The inspection started at 9:00 a.m., and the superintendent finally called it off at 8:00 p.m. Dan and his wife had brought food to eat during the inspection, but the superintendent went hungry. I admired the superintendent's commitment in trying to turn a thoroughly obnoxious person into a satisfied customer. Still, I felt bad that he believed he was required to take that much abuse for a wonderfully built home in immaculate condition just so a greedy egomaniac could claim victory by extracting money he wasn't entitled to.

The superintendent asked if I'd meet with Dan and his wife to do another inspection the next day. I had never met Dan, but I was already disgusted with him. After what he had put the superintendent through just to gratify himself, I'd lost interest in the goal of making him a happy customer, but I still wanted to achieve the right outcome— the best possible resolution with everyone's dignity intact. Dan clearly had no respect for anyone else's dignity, but I couldn't allow that to be a factor in my approach. He had been created in God's image, just as I had been. That was the dignity I needed to honor even though some of his wiring appeared to have been out of use for a while. But I was not going to reward his hurtful behavior by giving him anything he was not entitled to.

We met at the home at noon. Sure enough, he started out by telling me he was a master negotiator who always got what he wanted. I felt anger build inside of me. I wanted to tell him I was glad to hear that because I ate two master negotiators every morning for breakfast. Instead, I told him that I appreciated his passion for his work but that we weren't there to negotiate. That part of the transaction was over, and we were here to inspect the home before they settled the next day. Then it started.

All the homes in that community had been sold, and the salesperson had left our company to work closer to home. The last homes were now being moved into, and Dan and his wife were among the final customers. Knowing that the salesperson was gone, Dan's approach was to accuse her of making false promises and misrepresentations and then to demand compensation. But I knew his claims were bogus. It was a low-class shakedown.

There was no reason for this to get complicated, so I just got on one track and stayed there: "Dan, we value your business, and we value you as a customer. We want you to enjoy many years of happiness in this home. And we've honored every commitment we made to you."

That time, the inspection didn't last eleven hours, but it did last four and a half hours. It didn't need to. I could have simply said, "Settle on this home tomorrow or you'll forfeit your deposit." There would've been nothing wrong with doing that. There have been times since that day when I've felt as though maybe that's what I should have done and not one thing more. There are certainly times when the best approach for a tough conversation is simply to convey a single message and declare the conversation over. But on that day, I felt my mission was to achieve the best possible resolution, and that included leaving Dan whole. Not because he was a customer. Not because he was spending a lot of money. Not for the possible referral business he might send in the future. Just in the hope that somehow Dan and I could both come out of this tough conversation better than we came into it.

This was certainly a different situation than my conversation years ago at boarding school with Andy. I felt genuine compassion for Andy, and I wanted to help him to love himself more. With Dan, I felt no compassion. Jesus would have, but I didn't. Still, I wanted to maintain his dignity even if he didn't. My conversation with Andy was for Andy. My conversation with Dan was more about a concept.

For four and a half hours, he accused, he threatened, he shouted, he insulted, and he lied. For four and a half hours, I said, "We value your business and we value you as a customer. We've honored every commitment we made to you."

Dan's wife was clearly on the hot seat to provide him with support, so she did. But she was uncomfortable in the role. After a while, she just started looking around in other rooms to stay out of the line of fire.

I never raised my voice. I never retaliated. I felt incredibly strong—totally unshakable. I felt so good about the situation that it took away my anger with Dan. I saw how much Dan needed to win and on his own terms. Since there was no way that could happen, I needed to figure out another way for him to win, especially with his wife there. I could help him win by making him feel valued—as a customer and as a person—and I could do it without rewarding his behavior. I could take his behavior out of play by not responding to it. I could just stick to my story—"We value you ... We've honored every commitment"—and still show I took him seriously as a human being. That approach enabled me to totally disengage emotionally because my pride was out of play.

During the third hour, I could see him beginning to lose steam. He still persisted trying one angle after another, but the threats stopped, the shouting stopped, the insults stopped, the accusations stopped. Only the lies continued. I actually did begin to feel the tiniest bit of compassion for him. I understood at that point that what was going on was his desire to fulfill a self-definition. I believe it was a self-definition that needed to be changed more than fulfilled, but that was out of my reach for that day. The best I could do was not allow his self-definition to be validated at anyone else's expense.

Four and a half hours was enough. I finally said,
"Dan, I've given you four and a half hours because I feel
I have a responsibility to you—as a valued customer and
as a person. But I have responsibilities to a lot of other
people too, and I need to turn my attention to those. So
I have to say for the final time that we've honored every
commitment we've made to you. I need you to tell me if
you're going to honor the commitment you've made to us. If
you are, I need you to be at settlement tomorrow morning
at ten—the scheduled time. If you're not going to honor
your commitment, I need you to look me in the eye right
now and tell me so I can call the attorney and cancel it."

He settled. But there was no transformation. He began
all over again with the customer service department, but
we nipped that in the bud.

Was this tough conversation worth four and a half
hours? Was it worth anything?

Let me first address the four-plus hour issue. Someone
else could have accomplished what I accomplished (and to
this day I'm not sure what that was) in less time than I
did. Perhaps they could have done more. In any event, one
of the reasons I took so long was for the sake of caution,
which may not have been necessary. Caution is often
not necessary, but sometimes, we don't know until we're
through it.

Another reason I hung in there is that I believe we can
be most effective in tough conversations if we tailor our
style to our natural strengths. I tend to be the tortoise,
not the hare. In high school, I was a cross-country
runner, not a sprinter. I tended to finish faster than I
started. In all-night poker games at college, I had my
most success between 4:00 a.m. and 7:00 a.m. I've always

been drawn more to endurance than to speed, so I apply that temperament to tough conversations. Someone who comes out of the gate faster by nature than I do would probably do just as well more quickly. Sometimes, I take too long.

I once had an employee who caused problems with her poor administrative skills. It took me a year to solve the problem when it probably should have taken somewhere between an hour and a week. It was an inappropriate use of patience that I now look back on as avoidance (although it didn't feel like that at the time). I wouldn't make that same mistake today.

Another time, my patience with an employee who struggled with his professional identity was in fact transformative. It was similar to the Andy situation at boarding school, and it produced similar results.

So there are times when I would move more quickly now than when I was handling a tough conversation (or series of them) for the first time. But in the case of Dan, something told me to keep his dignity front and center no matter what, regardless of the result. It was just something in my spirit, and I was trusting its source. Tough conversations are not about the speed but about the spirit.

Sometimes, you do something entirely for the result, and other times, you do it just to do it. We won't always get the result we hope for, and we won't always be transformative. I got the result I hoped for. I have no evidence that the incident blessed Dan, but I believe the conversation was worth it, all four and a half hours. Tough conversations are sometimes like that.

Finding Our Position of Strength

The experience with Dan stays with me not so much for its result, which on the surface seems nothing more than getting him to honor his contract. It stays with me because of the dynamics and principles involved that relate to so many kinds of tough conversations.

This man who called himself a master negotiator clearly revered intimidation as the tactic of choice for getting what he wanted. Assuming he was even half as successful as he claimed to be, he must have had decent results with his approach since he stuck with it, and he was buying a pretty expensive house. The notion of "winning through intimidation" has had a large following for a long time, but Dan had projected so little substance. The profound fear he radiated was always so very close to the surface right from the beginning. This was what made me realize how important it was for me to maintain his dignity in this tough conversation. In his case, that dignity was very fragile.

Trying to win through intimidation has maintained its popularity because it often appears to work, at least for the moment. You see it in negotiations, and you see it in management. But how many of history's most *admired* leaders have been known for being intimidating? To the extent that the greatest leaders do intimidate, it's "intimidation" in the sense of inspiring respectful awe more than engaging in bullying behavior.

What exactly is the fear that drives the desire to win through intimidation? Sometimes, it's the fear of not being taken seriously. Other times, it's the fear of losing—of not achieving a desired outcome or having something taken away. For the most part, it's the fear that comes from pride.

Pride may be the world's centerpiece, but pride breeds fear. Let's see where Jesus leads us through His words and those of His followers to find our truest position of strength—for tough conversations and for life. We may be surprised!

God wants every one of His children to have a position of strength—righteous, godly, Christlike strength. He gave us the Bible to show us how to find that strength. His commands, wisdom, and stories were given to make us strong. He designed us so selfless love would make us strong and selfish fear would make us weak. When we live for God, we're strong. When we live for others, we're strong. When we live for ourselves, we're weak. That's just the way He wired us.

The world tells us to be aggressive and dominant in our tough conversations—to win, conquer, impress, overwhelm, and take. But where has that gotten us? We struggle with tough conversations because we're trying to develop a tough temperament by putting ourselves first. The unfortunate result is the fear that it won't work, and we live out that fear quite visibly when confronted by tough conversations.

Let's look at the alternative—God's way for us based on how He created us. From a worldly standpoint, one of the most bewildering passages in the Bible is the Beatitudes—a portion of Jesus' Sermon on the Mount. It tells where true strength comes from, and we can apply its principles successfully in tough conversations.

Beatitudes

Jesus personified the strength God wants us to have—strength built not on the artificial foundation of selfishness or bravado but on the sure foundation of love, selflessness, and humility. *The World Book Encyclopedia Dictionary* defines *beatitude* as "supreme blessedness or happiness; bliss." In His Beatitudes, Jesus described an extraordinary attitude of strength that enables us to be "blessed" as we bless others. These Beatitudes also apply to building a position of strength for tough conversations—a reliable, enduring strength that enables us to remain confident and steadfast as we provide positive influence to those we confront.

Consider these verses from Matthew 5 that apply most directly to tough conversations.

> Blessed are the meek, for they will inherit the earth. (Matthew 5:5)

> Blessed are the merciful, for they will be shown mercy. (Matthew 5:7)

> Blessed are the pure in heart, for they will see God. (Matthew 5:8)

> Blessed are the peacemakers, for they will be called sons of God. (Matthew 5:9)

The principles for engaging in tough conversations are really about so much more than just the conversations themselves. They reach into so many other areas of the life

God desires for us. The principles for gaining a position of strength in tough conversations are the same as those for gaining a position of strength in life. This is the case with the Beatitudes. They overturn our worldly, self-focused concept of what it takes to lead a successful life. When we first read them, they seem backward, but Jesus gave them to us so we could fulfill our potential in terms of the way He wired us. Now, we see that the desire for conquest in tough conversations—a desire rooted in insecurity and fear of loss—is really what's backward.

The four verses above are based on our natural, God-given wiring. They're part of the insight Jesus provided for how we can gain true strength and achieve true fulfillment. He emphasized the role of humility, mercy, goodness of heart, and the desire to provide peace as strengths that provide extraordinary blessings— inheriting the earth, receiving mercy, seeing God, and being called sons of God. Those are richer benefits than the best benefit package the world's most successful corporation could offer. Imagine entering a tough conversation with the kind of strength that comes from this spirit.

If we view tough conversations not as armed showdowns but as opportunities to offer blessings of lasting value to our adversaries, a surge of strength and energy rushes forth that we wouldn't otherwise experience. An entirely different kind of power—the power for which we are created—comes into play when we see tough conversations as special opportunities to be loving and courageous to do transformational good.

How did Jesus project His extraordinary strength? By living the verses above. Because those verses might sound too utopian by worldly standards to be practical for "real" life, He showed us how to live them. And while many don't follow Him or His ways, He remains the most admired, respected, and influential man ever. So maybe He was on to something after all.

By worldly standards, we might judge Him a failure because He never accumulated worldly wealth and was executed as a criminal, but that only confirms the unreliability of the world's standards for success. His reputation stands above everyone else's. His "career" has been scrutinized more than anyone else's, but there's not even the slightest hint He ever lied, sinned, or acted irrationally. He was who He said He was—the Son of God, sent among us to show us how to live at the highest level—to live the way God wired us.

The Sermon on the Mount was a tough conversation. Jesus was asking people to radically change much of what they thought, what they believed, and how they behaved from that day on for the rest of their lives. That's a pretty tough conversation, but He conducted that conversation on exactly the same terms He urged others to believe in. When the conversation ended, this was how the crowd responded.

> When Jesus had finished saying these things, the crowds were amazed at His teaching, because He taught as one who had authority, and not as their teachers of the law. (Matthew 7:28–29)

That is a position of strength in a tough conversation.

Jesus Wasn't the Only One

The apostle Paul never met Jesus in His mortal lifetime but in spiritual encounters (including visions) after Jesus' death and resurrection. Jesus lived in Paul as He lives in all who commit their lives to Him. Paul's life of following Jesus included many tough conversations—within the church, with adversaries of the church, with his own followers, with people he reported to, and with his own adversaries. After committing his life to Jesus, Paul grew into a man of extraordinary grace. Grace opens so many doors, especially in tough conversations.

Like Jesus, Paul was a man of profound strength and towering influence during his lifetime and in the two thousand years since. He's known not only for his remarkable life as a follower of Jesus but also for his extensive writing on how to apply to our own lives what Jesus taught and lived in His.

Below are five brief passages from letters Paul wrote with the heart of Jesus. In some cases, he wrote to encourage, in some to instruct, in some to praise, and in others to rebuke. He had many tough conversations face-to-face with individuals and with groups of all sizes. In some cases, his "tough conversations" were in writing.

Like Jesus, Paul never advocated being a doormat, nor did he endorse taking the easy way out, but his words express humility, compassion, kindness, gentleness, patience, forgiveness, and selflessness. If we apply these passages to gaining a position of strength in tough conversations, we will continue to see how different and how much stronger the Spirit of Jesus is than the spirit of the world. We will see how the position of strength we achieve with the heart of Jesus is so much more powerful than the position of strength the world promotes.

Be kind and compassionate to one another, forgiving each other, just as Christ forgave you. (Ephesians 4:32)

Be completely humble and gentle; be patient, bearing with one another in love. (Ephesians 4:2)

Bear with each other and forgive whatever grievances you may have against one another. Forgive us the Lord forgave you. (Colossians 3:13)

Carry each other's burdens, and in this way you will fulfill the law of Christ. (Galatians 6:2)

Let us not become weary in doing good; for at the proper time we will reap a harvest if we do not give up. (Galatians 6:9)

But can we really have the heart of Jesus, or was His heart reserved only for Him? Paul lived it, and so have many others. We look to Paul because he expressed so beautifully how Jesus lived in his own heart.

Let's apply what we've discussed to some worldly scenarios. I'll create four fictional situations to show how to create a position of strength for tough conversations. The principles I'll bring to life also apply beyond the workplace, but I'm sticking with the workplace setting so I can link the stories together more easily. Chapter 5 will offer examples in a wider range of situations. In each of these four examples, the "adversaries" are of the same sex. The principles I'll use would work the same for any combination of sexes in each of the examples, but I'm keeping it to one sex per story just to make sure the issue of sex cannot be an implied factor in the strategy either person is using.

Situation 1

I'll start out with a fairly easy one in the sense that both participants already adhere to the values I've been discussing for tough conversations. Here's the situation. Donna, a salesperson, has been lying to Nancy, her manager, for several weeks about the status of prospects she claims she has "working." Donna's desire to succeed is genuine, but she hasn't developed the ability she needs as quickly as she had hoped to, and Nancy is starting to ask questions.

Nancy doesn't understand why Donna hasn't made more sales in her first six months with the company. Donna is 25 percent below where Nancy believes she should be. Donna is trying to make Nancy believe she's doing better than she really is in the hope of buying time to develop the skills she needs. She's trying very hard, but her efforts are not paying off as well as they need to. The clock is ticking. The walls are closing in.

Donna knows what she's doing is dishonest, and it's bothering her a lot. So far, she's been able to justify it to herself with her certainty that she'll succeed and with the notion that she's not hurting anyone. She's claiming to have a number of prospects that are close to buying. A surge of sales could start popping any day, enough to catch her up for the entire six-month period. However, it's starting to haunt her that her deception isn't fair to Nancy. Nancy has been supportive, and she's been telling her boss what Donna has been telling her. Nancy's boss is starting to have doubts about Donna and Nancy. Donna begins to realize that it's more than just her own well-being that's at stake.

Donna wishes she'd been more honest from the start. She's just gotten herself into a bigger mess. She's not only falling short of her quota, she's also a liar. And it gets worse. One of Nancy's favorite sayings to her sales team has always been, "The only thing I won't forgive is dishonesty. If you fall short of your goal for the quarter, you'll get a second chance as long as you're doing everything else that's being asked of you. But one lie and you're gone." Nancy couldn't have been clearer that honesty was a nonnegotiable core value for being on her team.

Donna decides it's time to tell Nancy the truth and face the consequences. She makes an appointment to meet at Nancy's office. After pleasantries have been exchanged, Nancy asks, "What is it you wanted to talk about?" The moment of truth has arrived. Donna begins.

"Nancy, this is a new career for me, and I appreciate that you've given me a chance. You've continued to support me even when I've been coming up short. I know you've been taking heat on my account, and still you've kept believing in me. I couldn't be more fortunate than to be treated the way you've treated me. And it's not just me.

The whole team would follow you anywhere. I want so much to succeed, and I know I can, but I've done the one thing you've always said was unacceptable.

"I keep hoping the people I'm working with are going to buy. I've been trying to think positive and be optimistic. But I've come to admit that these great prospects I've been telling you about—the ones that are going to come through any day—I've been blowing smoke about them. They're real, but I need to face the truth. I need to tell the truth too. I'll be lucky to get any of them.

"I can't have you taking heat for me anymore when I haven't been straight with you. I just wanted so badly to succeed. I didn't want you to regret hiring me. But I've turned around and done the one thing that would make you regret hiring me most of all.

"I want to keep trying more than anything. I have a passion for this profession, for the product, for my customers. But I have further to go than I realized, and I need to own up to it."

Here's what Donna did.

- She saw the situation as an opportunity for transformation. She expressed sincere repentance, an important element in transformation. The *Oxford American Desk Dictionary* defines "repent" as feeling deep sorrow about one's actions; resolve not to continue. Donna showed that she was more concerned with improving than with defending herself or diminishing the seriousness of what she had done.

- She focused on Nancy's needs above her own. Nancy needed to know the truth so she could report it to her boss and make the best decision for the company. Nancy needed to maintain her good reputation and credibility as a manager with the rest of the company, and Donna respected those needs.

- She protected Nancy's dignity. She didn't blame her failure on lack of support or false expectations from Nancy. In fact, she expressed appreciation for Nancy's management style and affirmed the respect other employees had for her.
- Whatever fear Donna was experiencing, she took it out of the equation to give an honest account of what she had done wrong and why. This further validated her respect for Nancy. She dealt with Nancy in a spirit of love, not fear. She expressed compassion for Nancy in terms of the potential mess she was creating for her. She wanted to make sure Nancy didn't get into trouble on her account.
- She demonstrated that she took Nancy seriously by taking her values seriously.
- She was selfless.
- She was humble.
- She was in no way critical of Nancy or anyone else. She didn't make excuses such as, "Other people do things right under your nose that are worse than what I did."
- She made no attempt to undermine the innate position of strength that Nancy had in the conversation.

Donna's position of strength in this tough conversation became all the above.

Here's how Nancy responded.

"I can't say I'm not disappointed in you. I am. I believed what you were telling me all this time. But I also believe what you're telling me now.

"The reason I have the 'no second chances' rule is because a dishonest employee puts the company at risk, and it's unfair to the rest of the team. But today, you've convinced me you've done the last dishonest thing you'll ever do here. Sometimes, we all have to learn a lesson the hard way, but learning it is what matters.

"When I hired you, I believed you had what it took to succeed in this business once you got the hang of it, and I haven't seen anything that's changed my mind. We'll just have to focus harder on what it'll take for you to get there. I'll explain everything to my boss, and I'll tell him I want you to continue with us.

"Still, I want you to take twenty-four hours to make sure you can commit to me that I won't regret my decision to stand by you. Then I want you to tell me exactly how you're going to become the salesperson you want to be, and how long it will take, and what you need from me to get you there. Do we have a deal?"

It was a tough conversation for both of them. Nancy maintained the position of strength that was appropriate for her in much the same way Donna had.

- She saw the possibility of a profound transformation for Donna that could result from this conversation, and she valued the opportunity to encourage it while still upholding her and her company's standards.

- She focused on Donna's needs—not just the need to keep her job but also the important need to live out her repentance.
- She protected Donna's dignity without diminishing the seriousness of what Donna had done. She expressed her disapproval in an unmistakable but gentle and sensitive way. The quiet words, "I'm disappointed in you," can be a far more powerful rebuke than a vicious tirade.
- She took Donna seriously.
- She was selfless and humble in a way that was appropriate for her role in the conversation.
- She expressed disappointment without being judgmental.
- She didn't make Donna grovel.

Nancy's approach enabled her to project the appropriate position of strength without undermining Donna's. She asked Donna to take the situation seriously but didn't assert inappropriate dominance or indebtedness ("You owe me!").

Situation 2

Nick has become a lousy employee, and his manager, Mark, needs to put him on probation. Nick's attitude has been poor, his performance has been poor, and coworkers have complained that his behavior has become a distraction. Nick's been with the company for four years. He did a good job in the past and had gotten along with his coworkers. But he's been going downhill for the past three months, and his slide seems to be picking up speed. Mark schedules a meeting with Nick, and Nick shows up twelve minutes late. Mark is hopeful Nick can turn himself around. He intends to use this meeting to express his belief in Nick and to encourage Nick to live up to that belief. Mark will also need to explain in clear terms the consequences if Nick doesn't improve. But the conversation doesn't start off the way Mark had hoped.

"Nick, I'm putting you on probation today. It's clear something is bothering you, and I want to help you get past it so you can get back to the level of work you've done in the past. I assume this isn't coming as a surprise to you. This is the fifth time I've mentioned it, and I was gentle about it because I thought you were getting the message. But now I believe you haven't taken the issue seriously. I need for you to take it seriously. Can you talk about what's been going on that's affecting your work? Whatever it is has also been affecting the way you treat the people you work with, as I believe you know."

Mark hopes that his demeanor has struck the right balance of seriousness and support so that Nick will step up to the plate and admit he needs to improve. But that's not what happens. Instead, Nick jumps right into defensive mode.

"Are you saying somebody has a problem with me? If they do, they need to have the guts to tell me to my face and stop the backstabbing. You've got some real problems with some of your people, but you're coming after me instead because I'm an easier target."

Mark answers, "Nobody's stabbing you in the back, Nick. They're coming to me because their attempts to settle it with you didn't work. *I* have a problem with you, Mark, and *I'm* telling you to your face, just like you want. So far, it's not working very well."

"Well maybe if you'd show a little more appreciation, you'd get a better response. I've given four years of my life to this company, but when I get into a little slump, all you do is pull the rug out from under me. You call that supportive?"

"Nick, let's slow this down right now. First of all, you haven't *given* four years of your life, you've *exchanged* four years of work for four years of income just like everyone else. Second, saying I want to help you get past whatever's bothering you is not pulling the rug out from under you, I want to support your effort to get back on track with your work and with your friends here. But there needs to be an effort I can support."

"Don't call people who've have turned on me 'friends.'"

"We are your friends, Nick. People here care about you. I care about you. I want you to be successful. That's why I'm not firing you. That's why I still want you here as a member of my team—our team. You belong here if you still want to belong here."

"I don't know if I want to belong here or not."

The encounter reaches a turning point. Mark can lead the conversation toward Nick's termination if he wants to. Nick seems to be asking for it. But Mark isn't at that point yet; he still wants to inspire Nick to reach inside and rediscover what Mark believes is still there. Mark sees this as a critical moment in Nick's life, a critical opportunity to provide the influence, insight, and perspective that can help Nick find a part of himself he seems to have lost for reasons Mark doesn't yet understand.

Mark believes it's especially important to protect Nick's dignity, perhaps even from Nick himself. He wants to understand Nick's true needs and help Nick understand his own needs so they can be met. If a transformation for Nick is possible from this conversation, addressing the unmet needs pulling Nick down might be the key.

Mark knows this conversation is a high-stakes one for Nick's future even if Nick's vision is too blurred to see it. Nick needs to understand how serious Mark is about Nick's well-being. Mark also knows he must not let his sincere concern for Nick's well-being undermine his own position of strength in this conversation. Tough conversations are not about winning, but they're not about losing either. In this case, losing would be for Mark to let Nick's anger, resentment, self-pity, whatever it is, take control of the conversation. This is the time for Mark to be strong for Nick as well as for himself. Mark's strength will come from

- understanding and respecting Nick's needs,
- protecting Nick's dignity,
- setting correct expectations for what lies ahead,
- taking fear out of the equation on both sides, and
- speaking the truth in love.

This is what creates the potential for a transformational tough conversation. This is the ministry of tough conversations. Here's how Mark proceeded.

"Nick, right now, you're on probation because of your performance and behavior. That means that for the moment, the decision of whether you belong here is yours. If you want to know my opinion, I'd vote that you improve your performance and behavior and stay. I may not be expressing very much respect for your performance and behavior of the last three months, but I want to sincerely express my respect for who you are as a person, for who I know you can be, and for what I know you can accomplish. I've seen it, and I respect what I've seen. I mean that. I just wonder if something has happened to cause you to lose respect for yourself."

"I don't see why that has to be your business" is Nick's reply.

Another disappointment for Mark. He'd hoped for a better response. He believed the approach he was taking was the right one. But his position of strength was based on the same principles as it was before the conversation began. Mark responds.

"It doesn't. My business is the success of my team, and my responsibility to the team is to hold everyone to the team standard. The well-being each member of my team is something I sincerely care about, but it's not my business if you don't want it to be."

"Last month when Don screwed up, you didn't write him up."

"It was a different situation, but not a different standard. What I did with Don was right for reasons you don't know about. But even if I had been wrong then, it doesn't mean I'm not allowed to do it right the next time. We all have the right to improve. Which brings us back to the topic that *is* my business: I need to know where you stand on your own improvement. Are you for it or against it? Or would you like some time to think about it? Just remember that if you're for it, I'll be standing by your side."

"I want to think about it."

"That's an odd answer, but I made the offer, so I'll stand by it. Let's talk again tomorrow—three thirty—here."

Mark hadn't accomplished what he had hoped to. All he could do for the time being was hope that perhaps he'd accomplished even more. He could hope Nick would, upon reflection, appreciate what had just happened—that he had a manager who sincerely cared about him. Who cared enough to treat him with respect when Nick dared him not to. Who saw beyond his own pride to the good of his people. And who did it with enough strength to never give an inappropriate inch to appease Nick's selfishness. Mark could hope that within the next twenty-four hours, Nick would realize that if Mark believed he was worth salvaging, perhaps he really was.

Mark will not become Nick's "enabler" in tomorrow's conversation any more than he did today. If tomorrow, Nick says he is willing to "try," Mark will insist that he *commit*. He'll also make sure the expectations he sets in tomorrow's conversation are clear enough to make future conversations simpler. He'll lay out a plan for Nick to follow and insist that Nick commit to the plan. Nick will have to give his word. Nick will be playing for even higher stakes than he was today. Today was about Nick's career. After tomorrow, it will also be about his integrity.

Situation 3

We continue to move up the degree-of-difficulty scale, from a boss confronting an employee to an employee confronting a boss.

Angela's boss, Diane, treats her badly. Diane is rude, insulting, and occasionally threatening. Angela wondered if she was overreacting to Diane's behavior. Maybe Diane just has an outsized personality. Maybe Angela is too fragile. So Angela asked three of her coworkers how they felt about Diane. They described her as rude, mean, arrogant, hurtful, self-centered, and thoughtless. One of them told Angela to just laugh it off and not let Diane get to her. Another said that at least Diane was better than her last boss. The third said that something should be done but that she couldn't afford to take the risk. She also rationalized her reluctance by saying that Diane didn't have the authority to do any real harm anyway. However, she then said that maybe if she and Angela went to HR together ...

Angela didn't feel right about the HR idea except as a last resort. She believed that situations like this should be handled face-to-face first. She prepared thoughtfully for what she would say to Diane. At this point, she didn't want the issue to be about abuse of authority; she wanted it to be about improving a relationship. What was most extraordinary about her attitude was that she was more concerned about Diane's well-being than her own. Angela was well liked and widely respected. She was secure in herself, and she identified fear as an enemy that needed to be conquered to fully enjoy the fulfillment life offered.

The desire to get her working relationship with Diane to a healthier level was Angela's number-two reason for wanting to talk to Diane. Her number-one reason was that she felt Diane needed someone to talk honestly to her about the effect she was having on the people who worked for her and on the morale of the team as a whole. How else would she become the manager she was capable of becoming? Angela didn't know what Diane's true potential could be, but it had to be greater than who she was now. She trusted that if she treated Diane with dignity, Diane would soften. If Angela was wrong, at least she would have given Diane the opportunity, and someone needed to. Diane deserved that just as much as anyone else did.

Angela tried to imagine what need Diane must have to behave that way. She clearly needed the conversation Angela was anticipating, but there must be a deeper need driving her unpleasant behavior. Angela didn't know Diane well enough to be certain of what that need could be. But it did seem that Diane had a misdirected need for respect. Angela didn't fixate on the notion that respect was something that should be earned; she believed it was something that should be given and received.

Angela called Diane and asked if they could meet at Diane's office. Angela preferred to meet there because she felt Diane must feel insecure in her position and perhaps she'd be more secure in her office, and Angela wanted Diane to feel secure, comfortable, and confident. She didn't want Diane to feel threatened during the conversation. Angela's position of strength came from her sense of purpose in helping Diane and their relationship. If Diane wanted to become all she could be, Angela would be by her side to support her.

When they met, Diane immediately started the conversation awkwardly.

"So is there a problem?"

Angela didn't carry any anxiety into the meeting. She had given the meeting a lot of thought not in a spirit of worry but in a spirit of preparation. She wanted very much for the meeting to go well—for Diane as well as for herself. She had tried to anticipate all possibilities, and she had anticipated this one. She responded.

"There is something I wanted to talk about with you. I believe that as your employee, I have a commitment to your success as well as my own. I want us to be able to work well together. I want to work well with every member of our team. I believe you and I can work together better than we do, and I wanted to ask permission to discuss that with you."

"It looks like we're already discussing it, so I don't know why you're asking permission. Just say what you came in here to say. This isn't the only thing I have to do today."

"I'd like to be able to talk with you in a spirit of mutual respect. I want to support you, and I want to believe that you support me."

"So what do you want?"

"*I just told you what I want.*" Angela had decided that if Diane maintained an abrupt tone throughout the conversation, Angela would shift into that gear as well. Not to be reactive, but to keep the conversation on a level playing field.

"Is that it?"

"If you disagree with me about the importance of supporting each other in a spirit of mutual respect, then I guess that's it. If you agree, then I'd like for us to continue."

So far, Angela had anticipated everything Diane had said as being among the possibilities. She felt that the more thoroughly she anticipated, the stronger she would be. She'd feel confident she could handle whatever Diane threw at her without retaliating. Retaliation would derail the conversation, and Angela didn't want that. She envisioned positive resolution and hoped for transformation beyond what she could envision.

"Can you give me an example of what you're talking about?" Diane asked.

"My most recent example would be this conversation."

"Is my style too rough for you?"

"I believe your style is too rough for our team, including me."

"So you're telling me other people feel the way you do?"

"*Yes.*"

"*Who?*"

"If you had the kind of relationship with your team I'm talking about, you'd know. Everyone on the team wants that. It would make us a stronger team. It would make you a leader people would want to follow."

"Are they afraid of me?" Diane asked.

"I was wondering the same thing about you. Is that your reason for what you call your rough style—that you're afraid of something? If it is, there's no reason to be. If you want us by your side, all you have to do is tell us. Let us know that it's important to you, and we're there. We all hope it can be that way. We want you to succeed, and we want to be a part of it. You're our leader."

Diane didn't respond right away. Angela wanted to speak but chose to let silence run its course. We can do that when we're relaxed. Angela was relaxed, and she was beginning to see the possibility of a breakthrough with Diane. Maybe today, maybe not, but hopefully before too long.

Diane broke the silence.

"You probably weren't looking forward to this conversation, were you?"

"Actually I was—in a good way."

"I guess it's no secret that I appreciate directness. I guess if I'm going to dish it out, I need to be able to take it, so thanks for being direct. This may surprise you, but I actually do want to be a good leader. I guess we can all keep learning, right?"

"We'll all be learning right there with you."

When Angela chose the approach of "speaking the truth in love," she took her own fear out of play. It took away the desire to be accusatory or judgmental. It became easier for her to stay focused on Diane's needs, well-being, and dignity. Yet in a gentle, humble way, she made it clear she meant business.

In the end, perhaps Diane's greatest need was to be told, "We're not against you."

Situation 4

This situation has three characters. Will and Ken each manage a team in the same company. Will's team is outperforming Ken's and also has higher morale. The reason for both results is Will's superior leadership. Will is more respected than Ken, and Ken resents Will for it.

Ken was promoted into management when his predecessor was fired. The predecessor's name is Bobby, but Bobby doesn't play an active role in this story. The third character is Jeff. Jeff and Ken both worked for Bobby and had a chilly relationship with each other. Jeff had a better relationship with Bobby than Ken did. When Bobby was fired, Jeff was bummed out about it. When Ken was promoted over Jeff, Jeff was angry. He felt he deserved the job more than Ken, and he didn't want to work for Ken. But Jeff liked his job, earned good money, and was popular with his coworkers. He didn't want to leave. His only beef was with Ken, who Jeff believed had brown-nosed his way to the promotion. Jeff also was annoyed with the company for not promoting him, but for whatever reason, he chose to take it out on Ken more than on the company. He rationalized that he still belonged with the company and would get the job once Ken failed.

Jeff bad-mouthed Ken to other coworkers who were sympathetic to Jeff, and Ken had found out about that.

During a manager's meeting, the manager of another department, who also liked Will more than Ken, made a point of the fact that Will's team was outperforming Ken's. Ken looked at Will and asked, "Why don't I give you Jeff and then let's see who wins?"

The president who was running the meeting changed the subject.

After the meeting, Ken found Will alone and said, "Well, you sure came out smelling like a rose today."

Will smiled and replied, "Let's go get some lunch. My treat."

They took separate cars to the restaurant because they were going in different directions after lunch, so Will and Jeff both had some time to think. Will knew of Ken's resentment that Will had gained more respect. He didn't have much respect for Ken himself. But Will had been a manager longer, and he didn't want Ken to fail. He also didn't want Ken's team to be victimized by the resentment of a failing manager. Professionally speaking, Will imagined that maybe Ken was like a younger brother he didn't much care for but was still family, and older brothers helped younger brothers. It was in that spirit that Will invited Ken to lunch.

Will believed he needed to offer his help to Ken, and he sincerely hoped Ken would accept it. He wanted them to have a working relationship that would benefit both of them and hopefully their teams as well. But he didn't feel responsible for Ken's accepting his help. That would be up to Ken.

After they sat at their table, Will said, "I'm sorry about that comment Ed [the head of the other department] made in the meeting. It wasn't appropriate because he doesn't know all the factors."

"That's true," Ken said. "He doesn't know how Jeff brings the whole team down. Jeff's a troublemaker, and he needs to go away."

"You don't need that kind of problem. No manager does. Have you talked to Jeff?"

"About what?"

"About the situation," Will answered. "Have you told him he can't go on like that? Have you told him his attitude is hurting the team?"

"What for? He doesn't care about anyone but himself. He's dug his heels in. What he doesn't seem to get is that I can make his life a lot more miserable than he can make mine."

Will realized Jeff was the one causing the problem. But now he also realized that Ken's avoidance of the conversation he needed to have with Jeff was making the problem worse. He responded to Ken:

"That may be. But a lot of people are going to get caught in the crossfire. You can't let that happen. You need to be the one who leads the relationship."

"I don't see it that way," Ken said. "Aren't you the big 'Do what's right' guy? Well, he needs to do what's right. As you'd say, 'It's his responsibility.'"

Will felt good that Ken seemed to be watching the way he managed, but it seemed to be limited to selective listening. He replied.

"You're right, it is. But your responsibility is to lead the relationship. Assume that the reason you were promoted over Jeff was that the company thought you'd do a better job of leading relationships than he would."

"What would you do with Jeff?"

Ken's response showed Will the possibility of a breakthrough. Ken seemed to get it that Will was trying to help him.

"I'd sit down with him and address the issue directly. It could be that he's just wandered off into the tall grass where he's gotten so caught up in himself that he's lost sight of the big picture. He's not even thinking about the effect he's having on other people, or his responsibility to the team, or anything other than how much the world owes him because he wanted the management job but didn't get it. Plus, he lost his biggest advocate in the process. I'm not saying he's right to think that way. I'm just saying it happens. Our people get off-track sometimes. When we can help them find their way back, that's exciting! And people notice that kind of stuff. They want a leader who thinks that way."

"What would you say to him?" Ken asked. "I mean, I want to hear the exact words you'd use."

Will realized that now he was talking to Ken on two levels. He was talking to Ken about Jeff, but he was also talking to Ken about Ken. The conversation was getting closer to a breakthrough.

"I'd say, 'Jeff, I know having me as a manager wasn't your first choice, but I want you to know I'm sincerely committed to everyone on this team, and that includes you. You have that commitment from me. Please understand also that I have a responsibility to the team to create the best environment possible, and I need everyone's help to do that. That includes you. I've given you my commitment. Now I need yours.'

"Then I would stop talking and see where Jeff goes with that. If he thinks that sounds fair, I'd continue the conversation as long as it needs to continue. I'd tell Jeff what I valued about him and what I needed from him, and I'd ask him what he needed from me. I like to say to my people, 'If ever there's a time I'm not meeting your expectations of me as a manager, I want you to tell me, and if ever there's a time you're not meeting my expectations of you, I'll tell you. Is that fair?'

"If Jeff gives you resistance—if he's not on board— then I'd keep it simple. I'd say, 'Jeff, that doesn't meet the standards for this team, and if you're not meeting the standards, I'll fire you.' It's like you said, you can make his life more miserable than he can make yours. But that's the way I'd make that point. Are you comfortable with that?"

Will is having the tough conversation he needs to have with Ken in the context of the tough conversation Ken needs to have with Jeff. Will concludes.

"So, Ken, that's how I feel about management—about leadership. The company saw in you the ability to lead. That's why they gave you the promotion. But now's the moment of truth. Conversations like that are one of the hardest parts of management for a lot of people. They used to be for me. But I can tell you, it's one of the most rewarding parts too. I think you'll be more satisfied if you give Jeff an honest opportunity to lift himself up—a conscious choice—and if he makes the wrong choice, fire him. But if he makes the right one, it will do as much for you as it will for him. How does that sound to you?" "It sounds like the right thing to do," Ken said. "It's the same thing you just did for me, and I appreciate it. I can see why everyone says you're such a good manager. You're not afraid to pour your heart into it."

Themes

We cannot single-handedly determine the outcomes of tough conversations. We should not try to control them. We cannot even anticipate the potential that these encounters will offer. Too many factors are out of our control. Even Jesus didn't always achieve the result He hoped for. The adversary gets to choose how and when he or she will respond.

Having a position of strength in tough conversations doesn't mean having control of the conversation or its outcome. It means positioning yourself—your heart and your approach—to pursue the best possible outcome—maximizing whatever opportunity the encounter offers.

Donna, Mark, Angela, and Will each faced a difficult encounter. Each initiated an interaction he or she could have avoided by putting it off or by deciding not to have it at all. The four encounters had varying degrees of immediate success. In no case was the encounter the final resolution, but each conversation moved the situation forward to a better place than where it had begun. Each was a success in terms of maximizing the potential the conversation offered given the factors that put a final resolution out of reach for the moment. Each conversation either produced a breakthrough on the spot or made possible a breakthrough that would have been out of reach had the conversation not occurred. In no case did anyone regret the encounter. The success each conversation achieved resulted partly from the position of strength that Donna, Mark, Angela, and Will created and maintained. Here's how they did it.

- They showed respectful, sensitive concern for the needs, well-being, and dignity of the people they were confronting. They wanted their adversaries to remain whole and even better off to whatever extent possible.
- They had a purpose greater than their own self-interest, and this purpose provided calm strength.
- They conducted themselves not only with dignity but also with grace. They offered this grace to their adversaries. (Yet even when grace is offered, it's not always accepted.)
- They didn't merely try to appease those they confronted because they were committed to achieving a productive resolution.
- They were gentle yet steadfast.
- They were not antagonistic.
- They made no attempt to intimidate, dominate, or bully. They didn't need to because their strength was the real thing.
- They assumed their position of strength with humility. Their strength didn't come from aggressive behavior but from a spirit far more powerful. Their

position of strength was centered in their hearts, not in their behavior. This heart-centered strength empowered their behavior to radiate the peaceful, confident strength that is so appealing.

Each of these stories displayed people with a heart for tough conversations. In the next chapter, we'll dig deeper into what a heart for tough conversations means—and what it looks like. We'll see more dimensions of the heart of Jesus through the words He spoke and the words written by those He taught.

CHAPTER 4

A Heart for Tough Conversations

Success in tough conversations comes first from our hearts and second from our skills. The right heart makes the right skills come more naturally. In the last chapter, we redefined the concept of a position of strength for tough conversations. By worldly standards, the concept of a strong position is innately egocentric—it revolves around us. But we have seen how self-centeredness is actually a position of weakness. A position of strength is rooted in a focus on something greater than ourselves. We've seen what a strong position looks like and sounds like in tough conversations. A heart that creates a position of strength in tough conversations also creates a position of strength in life. It's a heart in which love conquers fear. A heart for tough conversations is the heart of God—the heart of Jesus.

God took human form as Jesus to show us what His heart looks like. He wants us to live our lives with His heart. That's how He wired us. He created us in His image so He could have a close relationship with us. He wants to enjoy us, and He wants us to enjoy Him.

The Bible is the story of God's love for us. It describes the kind of relationship He wants to have with us and the way He wants us to love Him. Since this book is about how to have tough conversations with the heart of Jesus, we will limit our scope of the Bible to the New Testament. We will look at some more verses from Jesus and from those He taught that will help us be successful in tough conversations. But the implications of what we will learn touch every area of our lives.

Definition of Heart

The word *heart* has a number of definitions. Here are those that relate to this book from *The World Book Encyclopedia Dictionary.*

- The seat of one's inmost thoughts and secret feelings; soul; mind.
- Moral sense; conscience.
- The source of the emotions, especially of love or affection; devotion.
- Kindness; sympathy.
- Spirit; courage; enthusiasm; determination.
- The main part; vital or most important part; essence.

The way we live out each of these definitions for "heart" in our tough conversations plays a vital role in our ability to maximize the opportunities these occasions provide.

The Fruit of the Spirit

The apostle Paul was committed to living out the heart of Jesus in his life. He listed what he called the "fruit of the Spirit" (Galatians 5:22, and it's capital "S" because he was referring to the Holy Spirit). The source of the Holy Spirit is Jesus, and the Holy Spirit bears fruit in our lives that enables us to live powerfully and to have profound, positive influence on the world around us. Much of the heart for tough conversations that we're discussing in this book comes from the fruits Paul lists in his letter to the Galatians: "The fruit of the Spirit is love, joy, peace, patience, kindness, goodness, faithfulness, gentleness and self-control" (Galatians 5:22–23).

The fruits of the Spirit radiate magnificent strength. When you bring these virtues to a tough conversation, you give yourself and your adversary the strength to pursue whatever potential the conversation offers even if that potential is small or even if it only sets a better stage for the next encounter.

The first of the fruits Paul mentioned is love. We've said that love drives out fear and that achieving the best results from tough conversations requires us to speak the truth in love. But what exactly is the love that comes from the heart of Jesus? And is that the kind of love meant to be brought to a tough conversation? Perhaps the most famous passage in the Bible that directly describes the love that came forth from the heart of Jesus is a passage from Paul's first letter to the Corinthians, which is often read at weddings. Here's part of it.

> Love is patient, love is kind. It does not
> envy, it does not boast, it is not proud. It
> is not rude, it is not self-seeking, it is not
> easily angered, it keeps no record of wrongs.
> Love does not delight in evil but rejoices
> with the truth. It always protects, always
> trusts, always hopes, always perseveres.
> Love never fails. (1 Corinthians 13:4–8)

Here are five reasons why it's so important to enter tough conversations in the spirit of love these verses describe.

1. A heart of love is a heart of courage. "There is no fear in love. But perfect love drives out fear" (1 John 4:18).
2. It becomes easier for your adversaries to stay engaged so you can keep the conversation moving toward a positive resolution.
3. Your adversaries become more willing to hear you out.
4. Your adversaries feel more comfortable expressing their positions so you can understand their needs more fully.
5. Your adversaries might find your approach to the conversation appealing enough to adopt it for themselves.

One of the compelling aspects of tough conversations is how much our approach to them parallels our approach to life. When we consider how we handle difficult encounters, we see a reflection of how we handle so many of life's other challenges. The spirit in which we think about tough conversations, plan them, conduct them, and reflect on them reveals a lot about our spirit for life as a whole. If the fruits of the Spirit manifest themselves in our approach to tough conversations, they probably manifest themselves in other areas of our lives as well.

Let's take a closer look at some of the ways the heart of Jesus was revealed in the New Testament and how His heart helps us gain better results in tough conversations. Throughout his letters, the apostle Paul described how to live with the heart of Jesus. In his letter to the Colossians, he wrote,

> Clothe yourselves with compassion, kindness, humility, gentleness and patience. Bear with each other and forgive whatever grievances you may have against one another. Forgive as the Lord forgave you. And over all these virtues, put on love, which binds them all together in perfect unity. (Colossians 3:12–14)

In describing the spirit in which we are to treat one another, Paul described the spirit in which Jesus loved and treated others—the Spirit in which God loves us, having created us as His children in His image. Paul led us again to the theme of love—the love that conquers fear—the love through which we are to speak the truth. Being aware of Jesus' love for him and how He modeled His love visibly during His mortal life helped Paul gain clarity on the kind of love he desired to convey to others, a love far deeper than mere feelings of affection. Paul needed to receive and experience Jesus' love for him before he could effectively pass that love on to others. Jesus Himself said, "A new command I give to you: Love one another. As I have loved you, so you must love one another" (John 13:34–35). Let's zoom in on two dimensions of love mentioned in Paul's Colossians passage above that relate to grievances— compassion and forgiveness.

Compassion

A dictionary definition of *compassion* includes "the feeling for another's sorrow or hardship that leads to help" (*World Book Encyclopedia Dictionary*). The definition of *compassionate* includes "desiring to relieve another's suffering." Compassion is an active, not a passive concept. It stirs us to want to take helpful action, to provide relief. This is the nature of God's compassion, and we see it in the life of Jesus. In the Gospels, the word *compassion* appears frequently as Jesus heals, restores, and provides for the people He serves.

Paul's words above in his letter to the Colossians convey a Christlike spirit. They confront us with the truth that we often find it more difficult to show compassion to those who need it most when they need it most. Are we as willing to show compassion for someone we don't like or when it's inconvenient? It's easier to show compassion to someone we love, and easier still when we don't have to step out of our comfort zone or routine.

But Jesus lived by a different standard. He gave compassion to people who needed it and when they needed it regardless of the cost. He could have found many reasons not to show compassion especially as He was being rejected, abandoned, and crucified. And He knew in advance it was all going to happen! Still, He showed compassion selflessly and continuously. That's godly compassion. When we treat people with godly compassion, we see them through God's eyes. We treasure the good in them. We have a sincere desire to help them gain redemption even as we pursue our own. Redemption is a need we all share no matter how much we may try to suppress it.

To feel compassion for an adversary, we must see beyond ourselves and our own needs to the needs, well-being, and dignity of the adversary. This may sound like pure idealism, but it actually offers a pragmatic benefit in tough conversations. Inserting compassion in a difficult encounter deepens your connection with your adversary, and connections are an important part of making tough conversations successful.

When I say connection, I'm not talking about the connection you had with the adversary before the conversation began. I'm talking about the connection in the conversation itself. You can have a severe disconnect in your overall relationship with an adversary and still establish a powerful connection during a conversation. Likewise, you can have a profound, positive connection with adversaries prior to conversations and create disconnects during your conversations. The conversation is a self-contained opportunity to create the kind of connection that produces a favorable outcome. The kind of connection that's established through compassion in a tough conversation can be a game changer.

When you anticipate a tough conversation with a heart for relieving the suffering of your adversaries or helping them get to a better place (even when they are already in a better place than you or when you're suffering more than they are), your compassion can take the conversation to a higher level and a more productive outcome.

Forgiveness

Jesus' compassion includes forgiveness. As He hung on the cross, He said of those who crucified Him, "Father, forgive them, for they do not know what they are doing" (Luke 23:34).

God commands that we forgive because He forgives, and He wants us to be like Him. He also commands us to forgive because He created us to forgive. That's to say, He wired us so that we're stronger when we forgive. He designed us in such a way that when we're hurt, forgiving is our greatest victory because of the unique power in forgiveness for the forgiver as well as the forgiven. What extraordinary wiring that is! What genius it took to wire us that way!

Forgiveness empowers us with a strength that revenge never can. When we forgive adversaries, we free ourselves from their power—the power they derive from our anger and resentment. Even when they have authoritative power over us, they don't have the spiritual power over us they have when we don't forgive them. And ultimately, spiritual power is the most valuable kind. The fulfillment we experience from worldly power is fragile, fleeting. We may even see our worldly fear increase as our worldly power increases. Spiritual power is, on the other hand, deeper and more lasting; it's the kind of power through which we're strengthened because of our God-given inclination – our wiring.

When we choose not to forgive, we increase the adversary's power over us. We allow their offenses to eat away at us, making the effect of those offenses even worse. We increase and prolong our own suffering, which ironically increases the injustice of that suffering. We deprive ourselves of the freedom and peace that forgiveness provides.

Jesus tells us that mercy, like forgiveness, is a godly quality. He instructs us, "Be merciful, just as your Father is merciful" (Luke 6:36). Jesus tells us to forgive others because God has forgiven us, to be merciful to others because God has been merciful to us. Grace and mercy are two qualities of God He wants us to emulate to experience the miracle of His strength and power in us. The power to forgive is a mighty power indeed; it displays godly grace. Godly grace facilitates tough conversations in ways that few other qualities can. It's a grace that we can claim from God for ourselves and that we can pass on to others in tough conversations. We saw grace, forgiveness, mercy, and compassion conveyed in a variety of strong ways in the stories in our last chapter.

Jesus also reminds us to be aware of using double standards in dealing with others. This has direct implications for tough conversations. He spoke powerfully about this topic in a tough conversation of His own—a conversation in which He was teaching truths that were hard for many of His listeners to hear.

Why do you look at the speck of sawdust in your brother's eye and pay no attention to the plank in your own eye? How can you say to your brother, "Let me take the speck out of your eye," when all the time there is a plank in your own eye? You hypocrite, first take the plank out of your own eye, and then you will see clearly to remove the speck from your brother's eye. (Luke 6:41–42)

It's been said that we hate in others what we fear in ourselves. This is a possibility we have to be especially careful about when we're approaching a tough conversation with a critical or judgmental spirit. Jesus also said,

Do not judge [other people], and you will not be judged [by God]. Do not condemn, and you will not be condemned. Forgive and you will be forgiven. Give and it will be given to you … For with the measure you use, it will be measured to you. (Luke 6:37–38)

Jesus was sharing powerful insights for how to enter adversarial situations with the strength that comes from a selfless, peaceful spirit—a spirit in which perfect love drives out fear. This is the same spirit embodied in Paul's passage I quoted earlier. I'll bring that passage back once more as a summary of what we have discussed since then.

Clothe yourselves with compassion, kindness, humility, gentleness and patience. Bear with each other and forgive whatever grievances you may have against one another. Forgive as the Lord forgave you.

And over all these virtues, put on love, which binds them all together in perfect unity. (Colossians 3:12–14)

If we include among the highest purposes of tough conversations the opportunity to be vehicles of transformation, reconciliation, restoration, and redemption, we will see more clearly how important the qualities of compassion, forgiveness, mercy, and grace truly are.

Loving Our Enemies

Jesus raised the bar even higher for compassion and forgiveness when He told us to love our enemies. There's no spirit of weakness here. It isn't love in the sense of surrender but in the sense of compassion, kindness, humility, gentleness, and forgiveness —powerful ingredients to carry into a tough conversation.

Here is how Jesus taught us to treat enemies when we're living in the strength of God's heart.

Love your enemies, do good to those who hate you, bless those who curse you, pray for those who mistreat you ... Do to others as you would have them do to you. If you love those who love you, what credit is that to you? Even "sinners" love those who love them. And if you do good to those who are good to you, what credit is that to you? Even "sinners" do that ... But love your enemies,

do good to them ... Then your reward will
be great, and you will be sons of the Most
High, because He is kind to the ungrateful
and wicked. Be merciful, just as your Father
is merciful. (Luke 6:27–36)

This is living the real heart of the real God in the
real world. If you can encounter your most threatening
enemy in a spirit of courage at the level described above
by Jesus, you'd be unstoppable! You'd be compelling.
You'd have influence. You'd enjoy accomplishments most
people wouldn't dare attempt for fear of enemies real and
imagined. Love conquers fear.

Approaching a tough conversation in the spirit of the
passage above opens a whole new horizon of possibilities
by breaking down the barriers that cause so many tough
conversations to be unproductive or to be avoided in the
first place. We're focused on the needs, dignity, and well-
being of the adversary as well as our own. They are more
receptive to and influenced by our selfless approach.
We take them more seriously, seeking to understand
their position more fully. Our agenda moves from self-
preservation to a mutually productive resolution. We're
alert to possibilities for transformation, redemption,
reconciliation, and restoration. We lead the conversation
to a higher level and achieve a more successful result.

The example Jesus set for us to follow was His
willingness to sacrifice for the good of others. He sought
to serve rather than to conquer. In His own words, "The
Son of Man did not come to be served, but to serve, and
to give His life as a ransom for many" (Matthew 20:28).

Most of our tough conversations will not require us to sacrifice our lives. What they do require us to sacrifice is pride—not pride in the sense of dignity but in the sense of self-interest. But that's good news because loss of self-interest in a tough conversation means loss of fear.

The virtues we're discussing here aren't manifested as powerfully when we love friends as when we love enemies. Some level of love is expected with friendship, but the love we show to enemies is unconditional love, and it opens up a new realm of possibilities for transformation. Unconditional love offers us a new way to experience joy. It releases us from the bondage of anger, jealousy, and resentment.

We're now getting deep into a heart for transformation—for ourselves and for others. We're tapping into a different level of enriching spiritual power. Not every adversary will respond as you hope, but many will, and you will both be richly blessed in the process.

Getting Our Heads into the Game

Developing our *hearts* for tough conversations includes getting our *heads* into the right place as well. How should we think? What should we think about? Is there a list of bullet points for developing a mind-set for strength that matches a strong heart for tough conversations?

The apostle Paul gave a beautiful example of this mind-set in his letter to the Philippians.

> Whatever is true, whatever is noble, whatever
> is right, whatever is pure, whatever is lovely,

whatever is admirable—if anything is excellent or praiseworthy—think about such things. (Philippians 4:8)

Tough conversations sometimes set the stage for a battle between good and evil in our hearts. This battle often plays a larger role in confrontations than we realize. It's important to make sure our hearts and minds are in the right place for a tough conversation before we engage in it.

James, a brother of Jesus, made an astute observation in his letter in the Bible: "What causes fights and quarrels among you? Don't they come from your desires that battle within you?" (James 4:1).

The path we choose for a difficult encounter depends on what we do with the wisdom of Jesus expressed in the passages from Paul and James above. The outcome of the encounter can be determined by whether our hearts and minds are elevated to the level Paul describes or are trapped at the lower level of our internal conflicts about what we want. James followed the verse above by writing, "You want something but don't get it" (James 4:2).

What we want can be a source of strife in our hearts that plays out in our behavior toward others. In tough conversations, each participant can get caught in the crossfire of the internal battles of the other. The internal commotion that surfaces causes collateral damage in the conversation. We feel a need to take care of ourselves, we don't want to be taken advantage of, and we want the other person to accept the blame and apologize. We don't want to hurt the other person, or at least, we don't want to feel guilty for hurting them. We want control. We don't want to be on the losing end. We want others to agree with our terms or suggestions. We want them to see it our way. We don't want to be misunderstood. We don't want them to say bad things about us. We don't want to be weak. We want to be right. We want the other person to see we're right. We want to do the right thing, but we don't want to regret doing it. We don't know if we should even have the conversation at all.

And all this confusion is just about the conversation itself, not to mention all the other factors that may be lurking in the background. Our grievances with the adversary for things not related to the conversation. Past mistakes and regrets. Baggage left over from our grievances with others. Frustration or loss of confidence from previous losses or unfulfilled desires.

The good news is that we don't need to resolve all these issues to achieve a successful outcome; we just need to keep them out of play. But how do we *not* think about something? By thinking about something else instead.

The heart of Jesus focuses on what we can *bring* to the conversation, not what we can *take* from it. How we can lift others up, not tear them down. If we have a grievance, we should focus on how we can resolve the grievance, not avenge it. If we're issuing a rebuke, it's about how we can use the rebuke to restore, not conquer, the adversary. We must focus on how to help our adversaries toward redemption, because we all need it, not away from redemption because they don't deserve it.

We quarrel with others because we quarrel with ourselves. We hate in the adversary what we fear in ourselves. This doesn't mean we must resolve every internal conflict before we can engage in a tough conversation.

Quite the opposite. We acknowledge the conflicts so we can be aggressive in keeping them out of the conversation by focusing on something better. By willfully engaging the adversary with a mind focused, as Paul said, on what is true, noble, right, pure, lovely, admirable, excellent, and praiseworthy. By leaving no room in the conversation for the desires that battle within us.

A Heart for Encouragement

When we look beyond our own needs to the needs of our adversary, we find that one of the greatest gifts we can give in a tough conversation is the gift of encouragement. It's an unusual but magnificent opportunity to provide the kind of encouragement that can sometimes be transformative.

Jesus encouraged a small group of ordinary people to a level that enabled them to change the world, and His conversations with them frequently involved rebuking them. He also had to encourage them to follow Him into a perilous future with courage, joy, and grace.

The literal meaning of *encourage* is to "give courage to." Jesus used tough conversations to give extraordinary courage to His disciples—speaking the truth in love gently but steadfastly. Frequently, the tough conversations He had with them were during their times of doubt and the confusion and fear that accompanied it. How did Jesus' heart for encouragement work in real life?

- He saw the potential for transformation in each of them no matter what kind of past they came from. He believed in them.

- He consciously sought to give them the courage to live out their transformations.
- He took them and their needs seriously.
- He forgave them.
- He had compassion for them.
- He maintained their dignity even when correcting or rebuking them.
- He was continually seeking to raise the bar for them and then encouraging them to rise to the occasion by demonstrating His belief in them.
- He walked side by side with them, setting the right example by living the standard He taught.
- He set correct expectations, even when it might seem to threaten their courage, and then was sensitive to their need for reassurance.
- He took the position of servant to them (as in the case of washing their feet) to set the example of humility that was to become such an important part of their courage.
- He encouraged them to live their lives in a spirit of love for others and a spirit of purpose for lifting up those they encountered. He encouraged them to give to others the kind of love He was giving them. He knew this would provide them with the greatest courage of all no matter how severe the adversity. Perfect love drives out fear.

Jesus sometimes needed to have tough conversations with those who followed Him to address their pride, fear, doubt, or selfishness. He sometimes had to straighten their backs to face difficult times ahead. He saw each of these conversations as a powerful opportunity to provide positive influence.

Positive influence is one of the most precious gifts we can offer, and the right kind of encouragement is one of the richest forms of positive influence. Encouragement may seem out of place during conflict, yet that can be when it's especially valuable for the giver as well as the receiver. We are uplifted, strengthened, and energized by the encouragement of others. We also receive those same blessings when we encourage others. Offering the right kind of encouragement during conflict is an unexpected act of grace that can provide fertile soil for transformation.

Jesus was the greatest encourager ever, and He still is today through His Holy Spirit. One of the reasons His encouragement was so powerful is that His love was unconditional. Pride can make it hard to encourage people we don't like, especially when we're in an adversarial situation with them. Yet these can be the times when our encouragement provides the richest blessings, including magnificent energy, to ourselves as well as to others.

Naturally, we are not to encourage anyone in wrongdoing; we are to be encouragers, not enablers. Encouragement sometimes takes the form of "discouragement"—that is, discouraging someone from taking (or continuing on) a wrong path. James said in his epistle, "Whoever turns a sinner from the error of his way will save him from death and cover a multitude of sins" (James 5:20).

The purpose of encouragement is to strengthen, not weaken, the other person. Encouragement sometimes requires us to tell others to change their ways to achieve breakthroughs as when Jesus told the rich young man to take a step that would be hard for him but would help him get where he was trying to go. "If you want to be perfect, go, sell your possessions and give to the poor, and you will have treasure in heaven. Then come, follow me" (Matthew 19:21).

Jesus encouraged the rich young man in this tough conversation because He knew the man's stumbling block that was preventing him from fulfilling his purpose was his love of wealth. If the man's wealth had not been a problem, Jesus would have encouraged him differently. Providing the blessing of encouragement to another sometimes carries great responsibility. That's why we need to make sure we're focusing on the needs of the other person and taking those needs seriously.

Suppose every person on earth was committed to providing encouragement the way Jesus did. Life on earth would change completely! Providing encouragement is one way every human being can change the world, at least a little. One of the remarkable characteristics of encouragement is the potential for the ripple effect. If encouragement is consistently sustained, it will continue to spread. Encouragement is contagious. What if this contagion could become an epidemic? It would be the first epidemic in history that made people healthier.

Just being aware of the power of encouragement can empower each of us to be an agent of transformation. Maybe we will not change the entire course of history, but over the span of a lifetime (or even just a year), a consistent pattern of encouragement can reach far and improve many lives. Some of the people we encourage may not be profoundly blessed for reasons beyond our control, but many will be, and they will in turn bless others. The ripple effect of encouragement provides an extraordinary opportunity for each of us. It may be the most far-reaching gift we can offer because the potential for transformation that comes from encouragement is so enormous. A heart for encouragement includes a desire to

- be an agent of transformation,
- contribute to the redemption or restoration of another,
- be an agent of reconciliation,
- be an energy source to others,
- lift up the discouraged, and
- provide the right balance of encouragement and accountability.

When we're heading into an adversarial conversation, we need to make a conscious decision before it begins that our purpose will be to lift up rather than tear down the adversary. Paul, who faced many adversarial conversations himself, lived what he taught.

> Do not let any unwholesome talk come out of your mouths, but only what is helpful for building others up according to their needs, that it may benefit those who listen. (Ephesians 4:29)

Beware of the possibility of your own discouragement as well. Your efforts to lead a tough conversation to an ideal outcome will fail sometimes. All you can do is maximize the opportunity, and sometimes, the opportunity will turn out to be small. Don't let that kind of "failure" discourage your heart. Even Jesus' tough conversations turned people against Him at the ultimate cost of His life, but still, His heart for encouragement had the most profound, positive influence on the hearts of others of anyone who ever lived.

A Heart of Grace

A heart for tough conversations is a heart of grace, and Jesus showed us what God's heart of grace looked like. I'm using *heart* here as a word that covers attitude, spirit, temperament, and mind-set. Having the right heart—a heart of grace—makes tough conversations so much easier that it also makes anticipating them more enjoyable. They become an opportunity to be an instrument of blessing for another. Even when blessing your adversary may not sound like the ideal strategy going in, it provides the most rewarding outcome with the most profound sense of victory. We're all at our best and strongest when we're living for the well-being of others, and we're at our worst and weakest when we're living for the well-being of ourselves. It's just how we are wired.

We are created for grace if we can free ourselves from the temptation of forces that oppose grace—especially the kind of fear that results from putting ourselves first. The "need" to put ourselves first comes from "fear of man." If we're able to free ourselves from fear of man—if we're able to free ourselves from ourselves—to manifest grace to others, that's when we're able to feel satisfaction at its highest level. It's how we have been created in the image of God—the image Jesus came to show us.

If we take the right heart—a heart of grace—into tough conversations, it changes everything. Tough conversations take on a new meaning and a new range of possibilities—transformative possibilities—for the adversary and for you.

Another wonderful benefit of a heart of grace is that it makes it so much easier to develop the right skills for tough conversations. They come more naturally and make more sense. You feel more confident about your purpose and the results you will achieve, and your confidence becomes your strength.

What Does a Heart of Grace Look Like?

A heart of grace looks like Jesus. For the rest of this chapter, let's look at five elements of grace as Jesus taught and lived it that relate directly to tough conversations and how to get the best results from them. In the next chapter, I'll show how the ideas I have discussed throughout this book come to life in six examples of tough conversations.

- **Strength**

The kind of strength that is in the heart of Jesus is perfect for tough conversations—as much today as during His mortal lifetime. His strength embodied courage. Jesus taught for life in the real world today as well as for the eternal world of God's kingdom in heaven. In the context of today's world, courage is often the first thing we seek for a tough conversation. Jesus walked into whatever adversity He faced with a sense of purpose for confronting what needed to be confronted so He could lift up those who needed to be lifted up.

His belief in His purpose gave Him the courage to persevere even when that purpose demanded sacrifice. His purpose in serving God His Father sprang into action through His purpose to serve others. His strength came not from living for Himself but from living to serve others, meeting their needs, and protecting their well-being. And we're wired the same way He is.

While His courage could be seen in His desire to persevere and His willingness to sacrifice, it could also be seen in His self-control. He was not rude, not easily angered. He radiated peace—to friends and enemies— and He sought to bring peace to those He encountered. "Blessed are the peacemakers, for they will be called sons of God" (Matthew 5:9).

He lived strength through His heart, mouth, and actions no matter what circumstances surrounded Him.

- **Love**

Jesus lived for the purpose of love, and His strength in tough conversations came from that love. Because Jesus radiated love, He *always* radiated strength. Never weakness. Never fear. Love in tough conversations is never weak; it's always strong. That was why He never had to compromise what He knew was right during a difficult encounter and why we never have to either.

Jesus loved His enemies. His love for His enemies never caused Him to give in to anything wrong. It never kept Him from rebuking them. He loved them in the sense of trying to encourage them away from the wrong path and onto the right path. He wanted to encourage them to live out the good, not the evil, in them. He sought the good in others and sought to draw it out whether it was with His apostles, with strangers, or even with enemies. He demonstrated love in His appreciation for others. He demonstrated love through compassion (desire to take action to relieve the suffering of another), kindness, gentleness, and patience. And He demonstrated His loving heart of grace through His desire to bring about reconciliation, redemption, and transformation.

All these dimensions of the love Jesus lived and taught are attitudes that enable us to anticipate tough conversations with hope instead of anxiety and to lead them with strength instead of weakness.

- **Humility**

In the ethics of the world, meekness is often considered a characteristic of losers. But Jesus was not talking about losers when He said, "Blessed are the meek, for they shall inherit the earth" (Matthew 5:5).

Jesus personified godly humility—powerful humility. Grace revolves around the kind of humility Jesus taught and lived. Humility based on confidence, without the fear that causes defensiveness. Humility that produces sincerity, not a smoke screen of bravado to disguise vulnerability. Humility based on assurance, not on insecurity. Humility that empowers people to be concerned for the dignity, interests, and well-being of others as well as themselves. Humility that provides strength to use a tough conversation for encouragement instead of conquest.

Jesus' humility was based on the strength of serving instead of being served. He took other people seriously and valued their needs as much as His own. Even though He had a multitude of followers ready to serve Him, He made sure He served them as least as much. A desire to serve is a powerful strength for tough conversations.

Jesus modeled a kind of humility that was strong enough to be respectful, even to an enemy. A humility that was not boastful, not proud in the self-centered sense. Not self-seeking. Not envious.

This humility is where true power is found. Jesus' apostle Peter gave a profound insight into the powerful humility with which we are wired when he wrote, "All of you, clothe yourselves with humility toward one another, because 'God opposes the proud but gives grace to the humble'" (1 Peter 5:5, quoting Proverbs 3:34).

Worldly power is a charade compared to the power of Christlike humility. When you bring Christ's humility into a tough conversation, you position yourself to maximize the opportunity of the situation for yourself and for the other person as well. The ability to turn a lose-lose situation or a win-lose situation into a win-win situation is extraordinary power indeed—power filled with grace.

• **Mercy**

A heart of grace is driven by a desire to forgive, not judge. It is not weighed down by the lingering grievances that darken our spirits. It is not weakened by the perpetual resentment that depletes our energy. Instead, a heart of grace is energized by the desire to see others redeemed, restored, and transformed. It is itself uplifted as we seek to lift up others.

Mercy releases our hearts from the grip of torments in us that seek to pull us down. It energizes us in tough conversations by raising us above the need to avenge, which only disappoints us and leaves us empty. Mercy gives us the power to move forward and to bring others with us. Our satisfaction comes not from leaving them behind as we might think but by helping them to find a place where they can fulfill their potential as we also fulfill ours. This was the effect the mercy of Jesus had on those who were willing to receive it.

- **Truthfulness**

In tough conversations, truth is not merely the absence of a lie; it's speaking the truth in love. Telling the truth that needs to be told and when it needs to be told, not just when it feels comfortable. Telling the truth that will enable the adversary (as well as us) to move forward.

Truthfulness includes seeking the truth ourselves. It means loving the truth and rejoicing in it even when it's not what we want to hear.

When we're committed to a path of truth in tough conversations, our hearts remain uncluttered by self-serving distractions. We maintain a clarity that makes us bolder because our purpose is purer. We are not merely *telling* the truth to others, we are *sharing* the truth with them. When two adversaries share in this search for truth, the unexpected bond that can result is one of the unique golden opportunities a tough conversation can offer.

The foundation on which this truthfulness is built is sincerity. Sincerity is one of the greatest human virtues in terms of the number of other virtues that result from it.

Sincerity can be faked, but not for long. When insincerity reveals itself, a relationship quickly erodes. But genuine sincerity brings with it a grace that infuses everything else. We're wired to be drawn to sincerity in a powerful way. Even our respect for our enemies increases when we learn they're driven by selfless sincerity.

A heart of grace enables us to open and cherish the unexpected gifts that are so often hidden inside the mysteriously wrapped package of a tough conversation.

CHAPTER 5

What It Looks Like

In this chapter, six stories will bring to life the principles I've discussed throughout this book. The four stories in which I play a part are true (with fictitious names of course). The other two are hypothetical stories based on composites of true ones that illustrate additional points from previous chapters.

Alicia

I really blew it. I went into the conversation full of confidence, and I felt it was running smoothly. It suddenly exploded.

I was meeting with Alicia, a vice president of sales who had risen to her position without any sales experience. Her sales team had complained to me that she had been acting increasingly agitated and that things were getting "weird." They asked if I would speak with her and see if I could get to the bottom of it. I encouraged them to talk with her directly, but none of them was willing. They were concerned that Alicia would "go crazy" on them. She always seemed nice enough to me, and I couldn't figure out where all the drama was coming from. But some harsh words had been used to describe her, especially when she "went crazy."

I prepared very carefully for how I would present the concern. In addition to being sensitive to the likelihood of insecurity (she was an inexperienced manager supervising an experienced team), I also wanted to honor the request from each member of the team that I "be discreet," a request that came from fear of retaliation.

I began my meeting with Alicia by reviewing all the positive things I'd experienced during my week with the team, especially things that related to her strengths that were recognized by the team.

She asked, "Are there any areas where you think I can improve?" I suggested that if she developed her management style around her most respected qualities (which I described to her), the salespeople would respond more cooperatively. I had used this approach many times before with managers who were on the ropes, and it had always worked. But Alicia became furious and tore into me with a vengeance. It happened in an instant. I was stunned because I hadn't seen it coming at all.

She asked me who I thought I was. She told me that I had no idea what I was talking about and that I had no credibility. She said I was supposed to be helping her, but this was the last thing she needed—I was the last thing she needed—with all the stress she was under.

I'd seen the wonderful side of her that I knew her employees must have seen as well. I was suddenly seeing another side. I could also see the pain she was in, and my heart was breaking for her. I could see that the stress she mentioned had already pushed her to the brink and that what I thought was my gentle touch had turned out to be a brutal push. I sincerely felt as though I owed her an apology, so I gave her one.

"Alicia, I'm so very sorry. I didn't mean anything I said in a disrespectful way, and I don't have any disrespectful feelings toward you. But I deeply regret being so insensitive, and I wouldn't blame you at all if you told me to go home right now."

I wanted to say more, and I hoped somehow I'd get the chance. But right at that point, I felt the apology was what she needed and nothing more. I just waited for the ax to fall.

She surprised me a second time. She burst into tears. And that's exactly what she needed to do. I thought I'd just sit quietly until Alicia had a chance to talk first. Then I had the feeling she was so overwhelmed that she didn't know what to say, so I went ahead.

"The stress is hard, isn't it?" I said.

"It's horrible!" she answered. "It's awful! And it never stops! It just keeps coming at me!"

"Is there anything I can do to help you? That's what I'm here for and what I'd love to do." I realized I was being paid to already know the right answer to the question I'd just asked, but it was time to stop being the expert—the talker—and become the human being—the listener. I put my agenda on the shelf and tried to tap into hers.

"I'm sorry about what I said too," Alicia finally said. "You're wonderful at what you do, but I'm not sure there's anything you can do for me."

I thought she was going to say something more, but she didn't. I asked, "What makes you say that?"

"I know I'm not a great manager, but I'm not sure I want to get any better at a job I'll always hate no matter how good I become."

"Well suppose instead of talking about how to get better at it, we just talk about how to have more fun with it?"

And that's what we did. We focused on ways she could relax more and reduce her anxiety, which led to ways for her to interact more easily with the salespeople. They actually had no problem with her except when she was responding to them in a state of high stress, which I was now able to see firsthand. The conversation about interacting led to a conversation about being the kind of leader people wanted to follow and how much of what it took she already had.

I admitted to her that being on the receiving end of her stress could be a bit unnerving, especially to someone under her authority, but there was so much more about her that people liked than that they didn't like. We could figure out how to take the part they didn't like out of play. And we did.

Humans have a remarkable ability to transform if we're willing to tap into it that ability. Alicia was. Most of her problems with the salespeople went away, and her stress level dropped considerably. The one unsolvable problem was that the work just didn't interest her. She had a particular kind of creativity that was better suited to other pursuits. Perhaps the most important stress reducer she discovered was giving herself permission to be an imperfect but adequate manager until she found her destiny, which she did about nine months later. She also gave herself permission not to be a vice president, which can be hard to do. It's a pretty cool title, and it pays well. But she found a career that lit up her heart, and that's where she went.

One principle reinforced by my experience with Alicia was that a conversation can turn good after it turns bad. Don't give up too soon. A tough conversation is often a work in progress.

I'd been working with Alicia on a quarterly basis for about a year, but my relationship with her after that conversation became better than it had been before. She became a stronger, more-confident manager after that day, and I gained similar benefits as a consultant.

She gave more thought to the well-being of the people who worked for her, and they gave more thought to her as well. This opened up the communication channels beautifully and made everyone's life easier. She and the salespeople turned out to have one enemy in common—fear. They joined forces to conquer that enemy for their own good and for the good of each other.

I have to admit that when Alicia blew up at me, my immediate internal response was to wish the conversation were over along with my relationship with her. I guess that's kind of like running away, isn't it? But I knew I'd regret that later, so I switched gears and quickly recalled other conversations that had started out badly but turned out well. There have been more than a few.

What seemed to turn the tide was that Alicia and I simultaneously began thinking about what we liked about each other instead of what we didn't like. That made it easier for us to forgive each other. And we both realized we would regret the situation if we didn't fix it. She gets a gold star for sincerely wanting to improve as a manager, and I get one for focusing on her needs, well-being, and dignity. We wound up bringing out the best in each other, which I believe is one of the great opportunities a tough conversation provides.

Millie

I promoted Millie from sales assistant to full salesperson because I felt certain she was exactly the kind of salesperson people would want to buy a new home from. She was a sincere person with a servant's heart. She was genuinely interested in people and in helping them. It was easy to see she was entirely trustworthy. Customers bonded with her easily.

Beneath her gentle demeanor lay a profound strength that she hadn't tapped into as a sales assistant, but I could see it was there, and I was determined to help her find the confidence to trust in that strength. She needed to turn her inner strength into boldness, and I was sure she could do it.

As she consistently made her sales goals, her confidence continued to grow. But after five months, the breakthrough in boldness I'd been hoping for hadn't yet occurred. During her sixth month, I was working with her at her community when her construction superintendent came to her office to tell her a home she had sold had been flooded. A fluke accident had done significant damage to a home scheduled to close in three weeks. The repairs from the flood would delay the closing by an additional three weeks. The buyer, a single man named Paul, needed to be out of his current home in three weeks because his buyer needed to move into Paul's home two days after Paul's scheduled closing date on Millie's home. The superintendent said there was absolutely no way the new home could be finished in less than six weeks, and the buyer needed to be called. Millie knew she had two problems to confront when she called Paul. First was the problem of where he would live. Second was the fact that it was a flood. That's a problem that many buyers freak out about. So in addition to putting Paul out in the street, Millie would also have to face Paul's loss of confidence in the builder. Millie was grief stricken for her customer and panic stricken for herself. But she had just been handed exactly the opportunity she needed for her breakthrough.

She asked the superintendent what she should say about the fact that the delay had been due to a flood. He replied that there was no reason to tell the customer about the flood. Paul was from out of town, and the mess would be cleaned up before his next visit. She should just tell Paul that the delay had been caused by something else. He said this was the right approach because everything that had been damaged would be replaced. The home would be as good as had been promised and as good as if there had been no flood. That was entirely true. Nothing in the home would be compromised. The superintendent's point was that Paul should be spared the potentially traumatic details of something that would have no effect on Paul's quality of life in the home, which was also true.

She asked me what I thought she should say. I asked her what she thought was right.

"I know he's going to be upset enough about the delay," she answered, "because he's got to be out of his home, and I don't know where he's going to go. And the flood thing might send him into orbit. But I still don't feel right about telling him something that isn't true."

"So you want to tell him the truth about what really happened," I said.

"Yes I do."

"Okay," I said. "I know you feel tremendous compassion for Paul, so we need to figure out a way to tell him the truth with the compassion in your heart and then reassure him the home will be fine. Tell him we'll put him up in a hotel until his home is ready." In the home-building business, that's considered an appropriate remedy for this kind of unusual situation that's different from just a normal construction delay. The home had already reached the stage that we had given him a completion date we told him he could count on.

"The first thing we need to do," I said, "is to see Paul's home for ourselves so everything you tell him is something you've seen firsthand and understand thoroughly. Then we'll come back and make the call."

After we returned, I told Millie I wanted her to make the call before I left. I told her I'd sit with her if she wanted or I'd go into another room if she would feel more comfortable. She asked me to stay. We practiced making the call before she made it, but I could tell she was still very nervous. This would be the worst news she had ever delivered to a customer in her young career. She felt bad about the problem she was going to cause for him, and she was embarrassed by the reason for it. She feared we would come across as the gang that couldn't shoot straight. But she made the call.

When Paul answered, Millie greeted him and said, "I wish I were calling to give you some good news, but we ran into a problem that's going to cause a delay." She explained what had happened and that she had just been up to the home herself with the superintendent and a vice president of the company. She explained the problem and the solution. She apologized and told him we'd pay for the hotel. She said we really valued him as a customer, and she assured him everything would be right by the time he closed on it.

There was silence on her end. It was clear Paul was expressing extreme disappointment to say the least. I couldn't hear what he was saying, but I could tell he was speaking respectfully to her while also expressing frustration. I could tell she was feeling flustered. I signaled she was doing fine. We had discussed before that she just needed to be patient and respectful while he processed the news. Even if he responded badly, she was to continue to be sympathetic and respectful but to resist any additional demands for compensation. He didn't make any. He just asked questions—lots of questions.

As Millie answered one question after another, I saw her transformation occur right there in front of me. It was like a flower opening in time-lapse photography. Her confidence grew as she gave him answer after answer. Her own sincerity and compassion was saving the day. She really was "speaking the truth in love." She began to smile as she talked. She shifted her glance to me and stuck her thumb up. Something good had happened, but I wasn't sure what.

Her voice got lighter but not flippant. Her heart was right where it needed to be. She had compassion for Paul, and she felt responsible for the inconvenience that had happened on her "watch." She felt responsible corporately, but she knew she shouldn't feel guilty personally. She began to realize this was not a catastrophe, only an inconvenience, and he seemed to be realizing it as well.

She said, "Paul, thank you so much for being so understanding. We'll work to make this right." He said something, and then she said good-bye. The call was over.

Millie and I talked about the call for quite a while. It addition to making sure we were doing our best for the customer, we also wanted to reflect on what had happened to Millie. "That call feels like a life-changing experience for me," she said.

I was curious about what Paul had been saying. Millie told me that at first his heart had sunk. He was not just disappointed; he was also scared. There were two questions he repeated in his distress: "How could this have happened?" "What am I going to do now?" He also said, "I feel that this whole thing has been a huge mistake." It was during these comments that Millie's own anxiety hit its peak. She told me, "It made me sick to my stomach." But she kept envisioning a happy ending to the conversation no matter how unlikely it seemed. She stayed focused on treating Paul with dignity, respect, and compassion but without groveling.

During the call, I had heard Millie say, "I know this feels terrible, Paul. But we're starting on the fixes already, and when they're done, you'll be as happy with the home as you imagined when you bought it. You have my word on that, and I'm asking you to trust me even though the accident occurred. This can happen during construction sometimes, and it's better for it to happen before you move in than after. But I'll be in your home every day keeping an eye on the progress, and I'll call you as often as you'd like.

And we'll make sure your hotel is a comfortable one. We want you to love this home, and we want you to be happy here. I want you to be happy here. You trusted me when you bought this home, and I want to honor that trust."

That seemed to be a turning point for Paul. He realized he wasn't in it alone. He didn't have to fend for himself. The builder had gone from being an enemy to an ally.

After he asked a few more questions and was impressed Millie was prepared with answers, he said, "I have to say, I appreciate the way you handled this. I know this isn't your fault, and it's not much fun for you either. Thank you for being up-front with me. You're a straight shooter. And you're very kind. So what's the next step?" That was the moment when Millie stuck her thumb up.

Paul reciprocated the respect Millie gave him, so he didn't try to take advantage of the situation by squeezing more concessions out of her. The rest of the conversation focused on details of how the situation would play out. At one point, Paul said, "I know that when I look back on all this, I'll realize it wasn't the end of the world."

He'd gained enough reassurance to shift into a calmer perspective. That didn't happen because Millie gave him a pep talk or unloaded an arsenal of positive-thinking clichés; it happened because she expressed her heart for sharing his burden. He could sense she was caring more about him than herself. That's what caused him to pay her the compliments. It was as though he had expected her to play defense, make excuses, blame someone else, avoid responsibility, and leave him holding the bag. He was impressed by her grace.

This grace had always been one of Millie's defining characteristics. She learned a new way to show it that day. She experienced a magnificent breakthrough with a specific fear that had been holding her back—the fear of what would happen to her. This had been the source of her lack of confidence. It had kept her from asserting herself in a number of ways.

The solution she found in that conversation turned out to be the solution to many other challenges she faced as well. She developed confidence in the idea that if she approached an intimidating situation with a customer in a spirit of unselfish respect and patience—focusing more on the emotional needs of the customer than on her own—she would be taking an approach she believed in. From that belief would come her strength, and from that strength would come the best result the situation could offer.

Adrian and Doug

Adrian and Doug were best friends in high school. They went to the same college, and their treasured friendship continued there. After college, they went separate ways to pursue different careers. Even though they wound up far away from each other, they maintained their friendship by phone, e-mail, and occasional visits.

Over the next several years, Adrian left the company he worked for to start his own business. Doug stayed with the company he had joined. Adrian's company became viable during its second year. Doug was doing well enough, but the company he had joined began to stagnate, so it didn't look like much of a future for Doug. He had married and felt he needed a career with more potential. He and his wife, Susan, wanted to have children soon, and they hoped for a large family.

Adrian asked Doug to join his company. How cool it would be to build a company together! But they wouldn't be partners. Adrian was not looking for a partner, but it seemed like a win-win situation. Adrian had always been the risk-taking optimist of the two while Doug had been the cautious one. Adrian offered Doug the number-two position in his company with a handsome salary and a generous bonus structure. They both felt that together they'd be unstoppable! They had tremendous confidence in each other—and total trust.

Doug and Susan relocated, and it turned out as well as all three of them had hoped. Adrian's company continued to prosper, and he rewarded Doug generously. He paid Doug a higher bonus than Doug had expected and a bigger salary raise for his second year. Doug and Susan were thrilled with their lives, and they were grateful for how Adrian was treating them.

Greed, however, can sometimes creep into this kind of situation, and Doug began to grumble to Susan about not having the opportunity to become a partner. He had expressed his desire once to Adrian, but Adrian had said no. He told Doug he had been up-front about that from the beginning. Susan counseled Doug not to let greed grow into a grievance with Adrian. She didn't want him to spoil a situation that was already very good for everyone, and Doug agreed with her wisdom. He was far better off than he would have dreamed two years earlier.

Things continued to progress nicely through the second year—another wonderful bonus, another generous salary raise. Doug and Susan had their first child and bought a nice new home. Susan was able to quit her part-time job and be a full-time mom, just as she had hoped.

Early in his third year with Adrian, Doug had a great idea for a new product. He shared his idea with Adrian, who immediately jumped on it. Over the next two years, Doug's idea grew into the most profitable product in Adrian's company by far. In fact, 65 percent of the company's total revenue for their fourth year together came from Doug's idea.

Surprisingly, his bonus that year was smaller than the first three years, and his salary increase was the same percentage as the previous years. Doug was angry. He tried to control his anger by quietly explaining to Adrian that he was surprised by his small bonus and average pay raise. Doug had expected to be compensated in line with what he had contributed to the company with his brilliant idea. Adrian replied that Doug was not a partner and that he had paid Doug very generously from his first day. Adrian said it was not unreasonable for an employer to expect a high-paid employee to have one good idea in four years. He added that he was getting tired of Doug's repeated efforts to squeeze more money out of him especially considering how much he was earning. Doug blew his stack, and Adrian blew his. Doug shouted insults about Adrian's ego, stormed out, and slammed the door. He was through.

Adrian sent Doug an e-mail, but Doug didn't reply. He left a message on Doug's phone, but Doug ignored that too.

After three months, Doug had mixed feelings about what he had done. His best friend was gone. A great career opportunity was gone. He had made a life-changing decision in a fit of anger, shutting both his wife and his best friend out of the decision entirely. It was a decision that had hurt everyone.

Susan asked Doug to resolve his differences with Adrian even if he never went back to work for him, but Doug was too angry, too hurt. He told Susan he wouldn't go crawling back when he knew he was right. Susan said it would not be crawling back; it would be making peace, which everyone needed. Doug said it would be crawling back.

The three months had not changed Doug's mind about believing he was right and Adrian was wrong, but he began to consider that maybe Susan was right too. Perhaps he should take the initiative to repair the damage regardless of who was right. But he didn't do it. He hadn't yet found a new job, and he didn't want to contact Adrian until he had one.

Two months later, he finally found a job, but it was in another city, so he and his family had to move again, this time to a smaller home in a less-appealing neighborhood. The new job paid about the same as the job he had before he had joined Adrian. He left without ever contacting Adrian. After that, reconciling with Adrian didn't seem to matter anymore. Plus, Doug was embarrassed.

Four years went by. Doug and Susan had a second child. Doug's job turned out okay, but nowhere near what he had with Adrian in terms of money or fulfillment. But it was what it was. The bright spot was Susan. As much as he had disappointed her by leaving Adrian, she never held it over him. She loved him. But Doug never found peace with the way it had ended with Adrian. He still believed he was right about Adrian taking advantage of him. But he grew to understand Adrian's position as well.

Doug kept reflecting on his friendship with Adrian—how much they meant to each other, and how much they had shared for so many years. He was sorry Adrian was gone, even sorrier than about blowing the career, although he was sorry about that too. He and Susan and their children and perhaps even Adrian had all paid a steep price for one prideful outburst. Even if he had been right about deserving a bigger reward for his idea, he finally understood he'd been wrong in other ways that were more important. Those were the wrongs he needed to make right. He needed to contact Adrian. Susan agreed.

Doug decided to reach out to Adrian by phone. He had no idea how Adrian would respond, but he wanted to be prepared for every possibility he could imagine because he didn't want to blow it again. Doug had grown to feel more confident in business than in friendship, so he prepared for his call to Adrian as though he were submitting a business proposal.

He began his preparation by listing his goals. Why was he making the call? What was he really hoping to accomplish? What was his vision of a happy ending to the call? He needed to be able to put his purpose into words for himself and possibly for Adrian. He wrestled for quite some time with the question of why he was really doing this. He came at the question from a number of angles, and the conclusion that he discovered shocked him.

He realized that the main reason he wanted to reach out to Adrian was to ask Adrian to forgive him. Doug hadn't seen that coming. He wasn't even sure where it had come from. Why did he want forgiveness? Was he feeling guilty? Is that what this was really about? The answer to these questions surprised him too and pleased him at the same time. He wanted to ask forgiveness for Adrian's sake more than for his own. He still cared deeply for Adrian, but he wouldn't grovel. That would defeat the purpose. The reason he would ask forgiveness is because he was looking at the situation from Adrian's point of view.

Over the years, Doug had come to believe that the tragic blowup four years earlier had been an honest disagreement. While Doug still believed he was right, looking at it through Adrian's eyes helped him understand how Adrian had arrived at his position too. He also understood how a neutral party might have a hard time deciding who was "more" right. He would explain his new attitude to Adrian if Adrian gave him the chance. But what if he didn't?

What Doug really wanted most for himself was to reconcile with Adrian, but he realized Adrian had veto power. Reconciliation cannot occur if either party opposes it. So the next thing Doug needed to decide was what he would do if Adrian was hostile. Perhaps Adrian just wouldn't answer the phone or return the call just as Doug himself had done four years ago. If Adrian answered but was hostile, Doug decided he would be patient. He would explain his position. He would explain that the reason he was calling was to ask forgiveness. And the reason he was asking forgiveness was that, unlike four years ago, Adrian meant more to him than his own pride, and he was deeply sorry for however he may have hurt Adrian because of that pride. Doug would admit his selfishness. He would do his best to make things right to whatever extent he could. Once again, he was determined not to grovel, but this time, his determination wouldn't come from pride. It would come from his desire to restore the strengths, not the weaknesses, of their relationship.

Doug would talk to whatever extent Adrian was willing to listen. More important, he would listen as much as Adrian was willing to talk. He would be attentive to what was going on in Adrian's life, how Adrian was doing, how he was feeling—whatever he wanted to talk about.

Suppose Adrian asked why Doug had never called him until then after Adrian had tried twice to reach him? Doug's answer would be, "A number of reasons, none of which seem very good right now. The thing is that I *am* calling now because you're the best friend I ever had." And if he hadn't asked for Adrian's forgiveness by that point in the conversation, he would do it then.

Doug tried to plan how he would respond in the extremely unlikely event that Adrian mentioned working together again. His response to that was something he couldn't plan, so he decided his planning was done. He made the call.

Adrian accepted the call. "Hello, Doug. I'm surprised to hear from you." Doug waited for a couple of seconds in case there was anything more, like, "but it's good to hear your voice."

When nothing more came, Doug replied, "Well, I'm glad you took my call. I've missed you and—"

Adrian cut him off. "I've kept track of you, Doug. I know what's going on with you. I know about your job. If you're trying to maneuver your way back into my company, spare us both. I don't want you."

Even though Doug had prepared for all possibilities, Adrian's words sent his stomach churning. He felt he'd been squashed like a cockroach. But then his preparation kicked back in. He'd stay patient. This call was supposed to be for Adrian more than for Doug, so Doug would stick with that program.

"That's not why I was calling." Doug wanted to keep going and explain why he was calling. But he waited a few seconds. He'd decided to give Adrian every opportunity to say whatever he wanted to say, and he would stay on that path.

After a few seconds, Adrian said, "I'm sorry, Doug. Why are you calling?" His tone was still cold but not quite as aggressive. If Adrian's tone was cautious or skeptical or defensive, that was understandable. In their last conversation, Doug had been much worse than that.

"Because I've missed you," Doug answered. "You're the best friend I ever had, and I let other crap get in the way of that. It's been the biggest loss in my life so far, and I could've prevented it. But I didn't. I let it happen. Perhaps I made it happen. But I wanted to ask you to forgive me for doing that. If I could do it again, I would handle it differently, but I can't. All I can do is ask if you can forgive me. That's why I called. And it's good to hear your voice."

Adrian went quiet, and the quiet was brutal. But if Adrian needed time to gather his thoughts, that was what was important right at that point.

Adrian finally said, "You hurt me a lot, Doug."

"I hurt us both a lot," Doug replied.

"Why now?" Adrian asked. "Why're you calling now?"

"I should have called before now," Doug answered. "I should have called you back when you reached out to me after the blowup. I just didn't. But thank you for taking my call today."

Doug could feel the call reaching a turning point. He would soon find out if Adrian was interested in restoring their friendship or not.

Again, there were several seconds of silence before Adrian said, "You're welcome. So how are you doing?"

Doug brought Adrian up to date and learned Adrian had gotten married two years previously. No kids yet, but they were hoping. Adrian also brought Doug up to date on his company but in a gracious way. No bragging, no nose-rubbing.

Doug replied with a pleasant memory he had from an occasion when they worked together and then another from college. Adrian suddenly interrupted. "Doug, I'm going to have to wrap this up. I've got a meeting to go to."

"Oh, okay," Doug said, somewhat flustered. "Well, it was really good to talk to you. I'd like to hear more. Can I call again?"

"Sure," Adrian said. "Call me." He hung up.

Doug was a little disappointed, but it was a step—a good step. And it looked like there would be another step. Doug was disappointed that the call had ended abruptly and that Adrian had not actually told him he forgave him. The call never became as warm as he hoped it would, but it wound up much better than it had started out. Doug just needed to focus on what he *had* accomplished, not on what he hadn't. He decided to send a follow-up e-mail right away to tell Adrian how much it had meant to talk with him and how much he looked forward to next time. Doug was excited about the possibilities the next call offered.

Patrick

After I had given a speech on conquering fear, an executive vice president named Patrick came up to me during the mingling time and asked if he could make an appointment to meet with me one-on-one. "What you talked about today is the biggest challenge of my career. I feel overwhelmed with fear. The biggest problem is that I realize my fear isn't just affecting me, it's affecting the people who work for me. I can't let that go on. I've got to resolve this." I respected that he could be so candid with someone he had never met. I admired his determination to conquer this insidious enemy for the good of his employees as well as himself. I made an appointment to meet with him the next day.

That night, I reflected on how many times this topic had come up with managers I had consulted for over the years, but never so forthrightly. All the previous times, it had taken longer to get the topic of fear into the open.

In working as a consultant for managers and salespeople, I'd seen how many problems were related to tough conversations. Sometimes, the conversation caused the problem, and sometimes, it was a symptom of it. Sometimes, avoiding the conversation provided fertile soil for the problem to grow like weeds in a garden. No matter which of these situations was in play, the opportunity to engage in a tough conversation provided a potential turning point in the relationship. It often provided the ideal opportunity for a breakthrough.

What made the study of tough conversations so compelling to me was seeing the amazing connection between managers' abilities to engage successfully in these conversations and their overall reputation as leaders. The managers who handled tough conversations with grace were respected as leaders, while those who handled them rudely, defensively, or arrogantly were disrespected. Seeing this connection showed me that the ability to master tough conversations relates directly to the ability to master many of the other challenges of human interaction.

What was most exciting for me to see in the business environment was how managers' reputations would change as their approaches to tough conversations changed. When managers engaged in tough conversations more graciously, their reputations improved. In some cases, the change was amazing. They went from being ridiculed to being revered, from being scorned with contempt to being admired with affection. They grew from leaders whom people didn't want to follow to leaders they gladly followed. Tenuous management careers became resounding successes. Transformations were real and sometimes surprisingly fast.

Then I realized it wasn't just a management issue. It applied to coworkers of equal rank or in different departments. Indeed, the same principles worked for interactions between employees and customers. After that, I began to see it more visibly in friendships and family relationships as well. The reason I saw it more easily and frequently was because I had become more aware of it. People who were more comfortable in tough conversations were also more comfortable in other kinds of challenges that impact relationships. I was learning that a person's approach to tough conversations was actually a much more far-reaching topic than just the conversations themselves.

Patrick and I talked for a long time the next day. He was interested in hearing stories of other managers who had conquered the kinds of fears that plagued him. He was fascinated by the connection between his fears of tough conversations and his other fears. He realized that many of his own anxieties in management traced back to difficult conversations that he had had, or that he needed to have, or that he had avoided, or that were still awaiting him because he had postponed them. He realized that if he could learn to stop dreading tough conversations, he could learn to stop dreading almost everything else about management. And he knew the issue extended into other areas of his life too.

As much as he enjoyed the stories of others who shared his challenges, he was also a bullet-point kind of guy. He wanted the summary version, the bottom line. What were the core principles behind what I was telling him through my stories and my stream-of-consciousness narration? He needed to become a confident leader—and fast. He connected with the idea that the solutions to many of his problems (including some family issues that had plagued him in much the same way his leadership issues had) were conflict-related. He believed if he could figure out how to be confident in conversations with people he was struggling with, he could be confident in a lot of other situations too. He wanted to find the paradigm shift that would get him where he wanted to go, and that desire was what made him ask for some bullet points.

There were four ideas he latched on to easily. The wording I use today for these principles has evolved over the years as I've learned more about how perfectly the heart and teaching of Jesus and the words of His followers address the challenges of tough conversations. For my purposes in this book, I'll use my current wording for these principles, but the substance is the same as what I told Patrick. Here are the four ideas that were most helpful to Patrick.

1. Speak the truth in love.

This turned out to be exactly what Patrick had been wanting to do all along. In fact, it had always seemed to him the obvious way to lead. It was as though he didn't believe he had "permission" to lead that way. Permission from whom? From the world. He needed to be tough, forceful, fast, efficient, and demanding to be an executive in a national, publicly held corporation. He couldn't afford to squander his time with people who were causing him trouble. Ironically, it was these misdirected values of "strength" that were making him feel weak. He had begun to doubt if he was cut out for management. Then he realized the very thought of speaking the truth in love made him feel stronger.

I was at first surprised that he had latched on to this idea so easily. Then I realized it made total sense for the guy who had poured out his genuine heart and humanity so easily the day before.

2. Focus on the needs, well-being, and dignity of the "adversary."

Patrick never even questioned this one. As with the first idea, he simply needed permission to think this way.

The fact that God had already given him permission in the form of instruction to put others before himself in a tough conversation was all he needed. He didn't for a moment doubt the idea that if he entered a tough conversation focusing on the needs, well-being, and dignity of the adversary, his own needs, well-being, and dignity would take care of themselves. To him, that notion held more water than any other alternative he could think of. Even the secular world uses the expression, "What goes around comes around." What Jesus taught was for the real world, not just for the Christian church. The Christian church did not even exist during Jesus' lifetime.

3. You don't have to be an expert.

This idea was more surprising for Patrick. He assumed he would have to develop an entirely new set of skills to be the kind of leader who could command genuine respect during tough conversations. He was encouraged by the truth that the right heart makes the right skills come more easily. He realized he wouldn't need to go back to school for another degree. It's a skill we learn on the job. Just embracing the first two principles would give him the qualifications he needed to enter a tough conversation with confidence. But that idea still didn't give him the assurance he needed. What if he messed up anyway? The fourth principle he embraced was the one that provided the answer to his questions about the third.

4. Even if it looks like it's going badly, it can be turned around.

It's interesting that we tend to look at events that happen in the moment one of two ways. Either we view them as the end of the story or we view them as works in progress. The overwhelming majority of current events are works in progress. We aren't sure where they're really leading, but we often treat works in progress as though they're the end of the story. We look at mistakes as though they won't be corrected. If we humiliate ourselves, we think we'll stay humiliated. If someone gets angry with us, we think they'll stay angry. At the same time, we can look at the lives of others and see how bad things have often led to good things—good things that couldn't have happened unless the bad things had happened.

We need to look at tough conversations that way. We need to view a bad turn in the conversation in terms of how it can be redeemed. The most frequent alternative is some form of anger. Whether the anger is with our adversary or ourselves—whether it takes the form of hatred, shame, or frustration—it leads away from redemption, not toward it. But when our eyes are kept on the goal of redeeming a moment gone sour—in any encounter—it leads us back to focusing on the needs, well-being, and dignity of the adversary and on speaking the truth in love. We don't have to be experts at it; we only need to cherish it.

Patrick and I talked about the value of perseverance in tough conversations. We talked about how it can turn the tide of an encounter just as it can turn the tide of so many adversities. That led us into a discussion about the fruits of the Spirit that the apostle Paul had learned through his spiritual relationship with Jesus. All nine of them are such vital strategies for tough conversations as they are for life: love, joy, peace, patience, kindness, goodness, faithfulness, gentleness, and self-control. Patrick was profoundly inspired by the role that virtue plays in tough conversations. He sincerely desired to be a virtuous man, but he had grown cynical. His cynicism produced fear, and his fear produced cynicism. He now saw a way out of his spiral—a way that was perfect for him. It's perfect for a lot of people because of the way God wired us by creating us in His image.

The fruits of the Spirit are the most powerful way to connect with other people or to restore a connection that's been damaged. This was the perspective Patrick had been looking for, and he was thrilled that the author of the perspective was Jesus. He had found a way to conquer fear and be filled with the strength he was seeking.

It's interesting that managers would be the ones to experience fear in a difficult encounter with subordinates. You'd think it would be the subordinates who would be afraid because they're the ones who would seem to be more at risk. But this kind of fear involves much more than authority. It's about pride, the fear of appearing weak, of being undone or exposed, of not knowing what to do, of blowing it. This kind of fear transcends authority, and it goes both ways.

What Patrick discovered was that he could lead the way he always wanted to lead. It seemed so much easier because it was what had always been in his heart. But there had been interference; his wiring had been tampered with. However, the transition from fear to confidence turned out to be easy for Patrick. He was on a new path but one that seemed so familiar, so natural. He became calmer, more relaxed, more confident, less defensive, less agitated. He was leading with grace. Other people picked up on it. They expressed their appreciation to him, and they spread the word to others.

For the first time, Patrick felt he was dealing from strength. The heart of Jesus is a heart of strength. Patrick had been given permission to operate from a position of love instead of fear, which is all he had ever wanted when he first chose to pursue management. Love conquers fear.

What had started out as a conversation about fear in his upper-level management position soon zeroed in on the topic of specific conversations he had engaged in recently with difficult employees or conversations he needed to have. Patrick and I initially talked for a couple of hours, and then we had follow-up conversations periodically. His self-confidence continued to improve, as did his relationships and his enjoyment of his position. Since Patrick likes bullet points, I will finish up my story about him with a few bullet points summarizing the changes in him that came from taking a new approach to tough conversations.

- He was leading with grace. His grace manifested the fruits of the Spirit. Out of the fruits came positive influence, stronger leadership, increased respect, and a better reputation.
- He no longer needed to worry about himself—his own needs, dignity, and well-being—during tough conversations. His own needs took care of themselves when he focused on getting his adversaries where

they needed to go. This was true whether it was a disagreement with them, a grievance from them, or a reprimand to them.

- He became more relaxed.
- He became more humble.
- He expressed more appreciation of others.
- He went into the conversations with more optimism.
- He spoke more openly and welcomed other opinions more easily yet with no hint of weakness in his position.
- He gave people a more tangible sense that he was taking them seriously. They took this as an expression of respect, which they reciprocated. As they realized he was taking them seriously, they took him seriously in return.
- He became more concerned with achieving positive resolution and providing positive influence than with self-preservation.
- He became a source of encouragement instead of discouragement. He got rid of the harshness, cynicism, ridicule, and judgmentalism, all of which can be unconscious manifestations of anxiety.
- A few of his more difficult employees became easier to work with because they too felt confident with him. Some also became more productive.
- He took responsibility more easily.
- Even his eye contact improved during tough conversations.
- He also felt better equipped to handle some of the other people-related challenges in his life.

Patrick's changes created a momentum for him that took on a life of its own. He became the leader he always wanted to be.

Michelle and Beatrice

Michelle was twelve and Beatrice was ten when their Uncle Jimmy died. The sisters' parents invited Jimmy's widow, Aunt Judy, to come and live with the four of them. The girls' parents were devoted to their careers, so Aunt Judy became the person most responsible for attending to the young girls' day-to-day needs. The arrangement worked beautifully for everyone—no jealousy or disputes over responsibility interfered with the harmony of the family.

When Michelle graduated from college, she moved about an hour away to pursue a career. When Beatrice graduated, she didn't immediately have a career to pursue, so she moved back home. She got a part-time job in a department store while she searched for a career. She had majored in communications, but she couldn't decide what to do with it. She believed if she searched diligently, the right direction would reveal itself.

Eight months later, Aunt Judy was diagnosed with ALS—Lou Gehrig's disease. During the eighteen months that followed, Beatrice appreciated the flexibility her part-time job afforded her to care for the beloved aunt who had cared for her.

Before Aunt Judy had married Uncle Jimmy, she had been engaged to a very wealthy man who bought her a beautiful diamond necklace. But then he fell in love with someone else and married her. He never asked for the necklace back. He said it was a gift, not a loan. By the time Aunt Judy died, the necklace was insured for its appraised value, $300,000. Michelle had always loved that necklace not for its value, but for its beauty.

Jimmy was an insurance salesman, but his hobby was wood carving. He especially enjoyed carving small animals. Aunt Judy loved birds, so one year, he carved a bird a month in his private shop along with his other animals. He hid the birds away as he made them. Then at Christmas, Jimmy gave Judy one bird every day for the twelve days of Christmas. She loved them so much that he built a wooden stand for her to display them on. When Judy moved in with the family, she put the twelve birds on the stand in her bedroom. Beatrice cherished those birds and the story behind them almost as much as Judy had.

Jimmy and Judy were never able to have children, so when Judy died, she left most of what she had to her sister and brother-in-law, who had taken her in. But she also wanted to give something special to each of the girls— something she knew they would treasure. She left her necklace to Michelle and her birds to Beatrice.

Michelle was embarrassed that her gift was so much more extravagant than Beatrice's. But then she thought that maybe wise Aunt Judy had seen into the hearts of both girls. Perhaps she realized Michelle had always been the materialistic one while Beatrice had the gentle, compassionate heart. So Judy must have given to each according to what their hearts desired not based on a financial ledger sheet.

But Beatrice was crushed—and angry. Michelle was stunned by the bitterness of Beatrice's response.

One evening shortly after Aunt Judy's funeral, the four of them were having dinner and reminiscing about the wonderful years that Judy had lived with them. Beatrice burst into tears.

"I took care of her more than anyone else while she kept getting sicker and sicker," she said in a broken voice as the tears kept flowing. "No one could have taken better care of her than I did. And it didn't mean a thing to her."

None of the other three dared express what they were thinking: this wasn't the Beatrice they knew. But they all felt compassion for the way she was hurting. They took turns trying to comfort her. They reassured her that Aunt Judy had always expressed the depth of her gratitude for Beatrice's devoted care.

Beatrice was never mean or cold to Michelle, but Beatrice was not the way she used to be. Michelle would call home during the day on Beatrice's days off, hoping to catch her when both parents were at work. Beatrice would check the caller ID and not pick up if it was Michelle. When Michelle visited, Beatrice was civil but never loving. Everyone was uncomfortable with the change in the family atmosphere. Neither Michelle nor Beatrice attempted to get together alone. It became clear that Beatrice was not interested in making things better. Both parents encouraged her to talk with Michelle, but she just kept saying everything was fine, there was nothing to talk about. When either parent tried to dig deeper, Beatrice put up a wall.

This went on for months. Eventually, everyone retreated into avoidance mode, and Michelle's visits became less frequent.

Michelle realized that she would have to be the one to initiate a reconciliation, but she didn't know what to do. She'd done nothing wrong. Beatrice seemed to believe she was doing nothing wrong either. But Michelle was not willing to accept the "new normal." This had to change. It was disturbing to Michelle and to their parents. How could it not be disturbing to Beatrice as well?

Michelle finally left a message on the phone. "Beatrice, I'd really like to visit when it can be just us. Please call me."

Beatrice did call, and she agreed to meet at a restaurant on Saturday. Their mother had told Michelle that Beatrice had started dating someone, and Michelle couldn't wait to hear about it, so she decided to start off with that.

"Mom says you've met someone. What's he like?"

"He seems like a good guy," Beatrice answered.

"What's your favorite thing about him?"

Michelle wasn't just trying to break the ice. She loved her little sister. She always got excited when something made Beatrice happy, and it always broke her heart when something made her sad. She knew that living at home wasn't Beatrice's first choice, and she wanted to see her kid sister gain some traction in her life whenever the time was right. They chatted about the fellow for a while, and it was pleasant enough. Beatrice never asked anything about Michelle.

Michelle decided to take a step closer to the task at hand. She believed they needed to talk it through and try to close the gap that had grown between them. But she didn't want to come across like, "Okay, we both know why we're here. Let's get down to business." This was not about a task. It was about a relationship. It was about her sister's well-being. She didn't want her sister to feel hurt.

"I guess it's a lot different without Aunt Judy, especially for you," Michelle began. "You were the one who was always there for her. You gave her joy. And you gave her the strength to persevere. You were her angel. And you're probably the only one of us who could have done it."

"Thanks," Beatrice replied. Michelle had hoped for a longer answer, but she didn't get one. She wasn't hoping for anything grand. Grand wasn't Beatrice's style. It's just that Michelle meant every word of what she said, and she wanted Beatrice to feel the depth of her respect and gratitude. She wanted Beatrice to feel the love Michelle felt as she said those words.

"I think that's how she felt too," Michelle continued. "She knew you were God's gift to comfort her in those final difficult months—and there were a lot of them."

"Eighteen," Beatrice said. Again, that was it.

"I'm so proud of you. You've got gifts I really admire," Michelle said, "gifts that I know you didn't get from me, or even from Mom and Dad." Every word was the truth. She had always admired her younger sister. She realized as she was thinking about this get-together that she had never put her appreciation of Beatrice into words before, and the realization surprised her.

"Thanks," Beatrice said again. And again that was it.

Michelle believed the moment had come to say what needed to be said.

"Beatrice," she began. Michelle just wanted to say her sister's beautiful name. "I feel as though it hurt your feelings that Aunt Judy gave me the necklace. I just want you to know I'm not planning to sell it—ever. I honestly believe Aunt Judy was just trying to give us each something that would make us happy."

Beatrice finally spoke an entire sentence about the sensitive situation. "Maybe in her way she thought she was." "But you love those birds," Michelle said. "They're beautiful, and they were Uncle Jimmy's expression of love to Aunt Judy. They have a different kind of value than the necklace. That other guy spent a lot on the necklace, but he had more money than he knew what to do with. What Uncle Jimmy gave Aunt Judy was love, and that's the gift she passed on to you."

"I just don't understand how she could be so insensitive after all I did for her. She left you a fortune."

"She left us both a fortune, just a different kind of fortune."

"You see it one way, and I see it another."

Michelle began to believe that a shift in the conversation was needed and that she was the one who would have to initiate it. She was quickly trying to digest what was going on. She had expressed sincere interest in Beatrice in several ways during the conversation, but Beatrice hadn't reciprocated. Michelle had expressed compassion and love and respect, but Beatrice hadn't reciprocated that either. Michelle wanted to be careful not to start expressing grievances. It was her sister's well-being she was concerned about, not her own. Beatrice didn't need anything else to feel bad about. But Beatrice was digging herself deeper into a hole of her own making, and Michelle had to get her to stop digging. She had been speaking the truth in love, but it was time to start speaking a different truth—for Beatrice's sake, not for Michelle's. She needed to be sure to keep Beatrice's dignity intact, but she also believed she couldn't keep indulging her sister's self-centeredness.

"Beatrice, I think we need to give Aunt Judy the benefit of the doubt here. When was she ever insensitive to either of us before? There's no reason to believe she was being insensitive with her gifts to us. She probably believed in both of us enough to believe that neither of us would ever sell what she left us. She probably believed we would just treasure her gifts and then pass them on, because that's what she did. She always appreciated the compassion you gave her. She admired it. Where is it now?

"Everyone has been sensitive to you. I'm trying to reach out to you now. I'm interested in your new guy. I want us to have what we've always had, because you're my sister and I love you. I think this whole thing with the necklace has taken on a life of its own that would really hurt Aunt Judy's feelings."

There was so much more that Michelle wanted to say, but she suddenly decided it was time to stop talking. It was Beatrice's turn. Michelle needed to be the listener.

She was also aware that her efforts might fail. Reconciliation doesn't work if either party wants to sabotage it. All Michelle could do was try to help Beatrice get to a better place. At that point, Beatrice seemed trapped in a downward spiral of believing she was entitled to more than she had gotten. She was fixating on her rights, on what was owed to her.

Michelle could feel herself getting angry with Beatrice, and she could not give in to that. It would unravel everything she had hoped to accomplish. She had gotten into trouble with her anger before. She had learned from experience how easy it was for her to lose her sense of grace in this kind of situation, and she couldn't afford to lose it this time. Only one thing mattered—getting

Beatrice out of her spiral. She hoped she had gotten her sister to a point that she wanted to restore what they had once had as much as Michelle did. She had stayed strong and kept her cool. Any more could be overkill.

Beatrice came through.

"I don't know how I got so caught up in the money," she said. "Maybe I'm jealous that you have a good job and I don't. This job search has really gotten inside my head. I feel so broke. But that's no excuse for the way I've acted over the necklace. Thanks for finding a nice way to say, 'Get over yourself.' I needed somebody to say it.

"I'm sorry I've been distant. I appreciate you being my big sister now as much as ever. A big sister is just what I need right now. I didn't mean to insult Aunt Judy or you. She knew what she was doing giving you the necklace and me the birds. I'm happy for both of us."

Michelle was proud of her little sister once again. She was prepared for it to have taken longer or for Beatrice to respond poorly. She had decided if that happened, she would be patient, just like Aunt Judy had been with both of them.

Dennis

Dennis bought a townhome from me in a community where all the homes had brick fronts. The builder liked painted brick. He believed it would give the community an upscale feeling if one home in each building had painted brick. All the exteriors were preselected, so if you wanted painted brick, you had to choose the home that had been selected for it. Most customers felt differently than the builder about painted brick. They preferred the natural look of brick. They also didn't want the extra maintenance cost of repainting the brick. But the builder was right that some people in the upper brackets considered it a prestige feature. He had it on his own home.

Dennis hated painted brick. He thought it was stupid and ugly. He was a single guy, and he told me he'd rather show up for a date on a mule than bring a girl home to a house with painted brick. Man, did he hate it!

All the homes under construction had been sold, so the building he was buying in had not been started. He said he needed assurance that his home would not have painted brick. When I told him it wouldn't, he said he needed more assurance than that. I showed him the chart with the exteriors of all the homes. The painted brick would be two doors down. I assured him that the chart I had was the same chart the painter worked from, so there was no way his home could be painted. I promised to follow up with the superintendent and stay on top of the situation, which I did.

He still seemed nervous about the whole thing. He said, "I'm not sure you fully understand how much I hate painted brick." I said I believed I did, because his message had been frequent and emphatic. Then I made a regrettable statement: "I give you my word."

You've probably figured out where this story's headed. I've heard people say that the more you worry about something, the more likely it is to happen. Dennis turned out to be Exhibit A for that theory.

The hours of my sales office were 11:00 a.m. to 7:00 p.m. The construction people started at 7:00 a.m. This meant that the front of a townhome could be completely painted before I arrived. I knew that the home in Dennis's building would be painted that day, so I had pleaded with the superintendent one more time: please watch that building when the painter starts to make sure he paints the right home. The superintendent told me he was fed up with my whining and was tired of being talked to like he was an idiot. He told me I could get there at 7:00 and check it for myself, which in retrospect I should have done. What I saw when I got there at 10:45 made me sick to my stomach.

I know this incident doesn't live up to the dictionary definition of a crisis, but at the time it seemed like one—for two reasons. First, the customer had made it as clear as humanly possible how important this was to him. Second, I had given my word, so he chose my community over another one that had no painted brick. Mostly, I felt awful for the disappointment and sadness he was about to experience.

Moments like this don't feel like gifts at the time. They feel frustrating, humiliating, discouraging, and unfair. They are moments when the question "Why?" seems to have no answer. But I look back on this situation as one of many surprising gifts that bless me to this day. My problem at the time was that I saw the painted brick as the end of the story and not as a work in progress. I didn't have hope.

The first thing I did was call the owner of the company to explain the situation. He said I had three options. One was to refund Dennis's money and cancel his contract if he wanted to. I appreciated that the owner didn't want to hold Dennis to the contract even though he had a legal right to do so. Still, it would not unpaint the brick. The second option was I could move Dennis to a later home on the same terms even though prices had gone up. That also was a gracious gesture, although the next available home would not be finished for six months, which would not work for Dennis. The third option was for Dennis to decide that the painted brick was acceptable. The owner didn't offer any financial compensation for Dennis to accept the brick.

I pondered my next step. I saw two possibilities. I could wait until Dennis's next visit and let him see it for himself. Or I could call him immediately so I could be sure to reach him before he saw it. The second approach seemed better, so I called him.

The "salesman" in me was nowhere to be found. There was no positive spin—no good news and bad news. There was only bad news. We had screwed up, and we would get off scot-free while Dennis would be left holding the bag. As soon as he answered my call, I knew I was only seconds away from breaking his heart. Yet I wanted to get the whole mess out into the open as quickly as possible.

"Hi, Dennis, this is Rich Tiller. I'm afraid I'm calling with some bad news."

"You painted the brick."

I was stunned. How could he have seen it already? It was still only 11:15.

"How did you know?" I asked.

"I knew this would happen. I just knew it." So he hadn't seen it after all.

It made me sick that he was right—that he had been right all along not to trust me.

"I'm just so sorry," I said. "I talked to the superintendent yesterday. I was sure everything would be fine. I knew the painting was today, and I should have gotten here before the painter—"

Before I could get any further, he said, "I can't believe this has happened."

"I know. I'm so sorry. I should have come out earlier to make sure. I know how important this was to you and how concerned you were that this would happen. And you were right all along. I'm so sorry."

"I just can't believe this happened."

"I know. I am so sorry."

"I just can't believe it."

I realized there was no point in continuing to tell him how sorry I was. I felt like I was listening to one of those old records where the needle used to get stuck in the groove. I just needed to be quiet and let him decide where he wanted to go next.

"What am I going to do?" he finally said.

I explained the three options, and then I added a fourth. "The only other thing I can do is to say that if you decide you can live with the painted brick, then you're more entitled to my commission than I am." I gave him the figure and said, "And I can have the check made out to you instead of me. I wish I could do more, but that's the only thing I can give you to say how sorry I am for not doing my job."

He didn't say anything. I didn't either, because I didn't have anything more to say. I just felt bad for him.

He finally said, "How bad does it look?" My office sat up on a hill so I could see the entire community through my window, and his home faced the street closest to my office.

"I can tell you how it looks to me," I answered. "But what's important is how it looks to you."

"I know. But what do you think?"

"I think it looks terrific, but I'm in the business. I'm trained to think painted brick is a prestige look. So I can tell you I think it looks like a million bucks—literally. Homes in this area that cost a million bucks often have painted brick. The owner of our company lives in a million-dollar home, and his home has painted brick. So I like the look, and I especially like that color." Every word of that was the truth.

"Seriously?" Dennis asked.

"Seriously."

"Well, I'm really disappointed. But I'll come out at lunch to look at it."

"Do you want me to meet you at the house?"

"No. I just want to see it myself and let it sink in."

About an hour later, I saw him drive up and get out of his car. As he stood in front of his home, his shoulders slumped. After staring at the home for a while, he looked at the ground and shook his head. He looked up and stared some more at his townhouse. He got into his car and drove away. He didn't stop by my office. Not good.

At about 2:00, I called him again.

"Hi, Dennis. It's Rich. I saw you stop by, and I wanted to follow up to see what you thought."

He didn't answer for a few seconds. A few very long seconds. He said, "I'll take the painted brick."

I was dumbfounded. "Really?"

"Yeah."

"Are you really okay with it?"

"It's growing on me. It's just a really different way of thinking for me."

"I'm so glad. I hope you get to where you think it's the most beautiful home in the building."

"I'm not quite there yet," was Dennis's response to that. "Who knows? It's just a different way of thinking. But thanks for not just telling me to get over it. You took me seriously, and that helped a lot."

"Well, thanks for saying that. You've been incredibly gracious about this. I'll make sure the check for my commission is made out to you at settlement, and this time, I'll come over and see the check for myself before the settlement starts."

"You keep your commission. You earned it."

In some ways, this story is similar to the earlier one about Millie, but I wanted to tell them separately. For one thing, I was an observer in one and a participant in the other so the stories come from different angles. Another difference was that in this case, the "adversary" changed his way of thinking by gaining a new perspective. This change seemed to come from trust as well as from learning a new way to look at something. The fact that he trusted me was a huge takeaway for me in this story because I had betrayed his trust. Dennis taught me never to lose hope that trust can be restored and that new perspectives can make a big difference when trust is in play.

The Dennis story happened about thirty years before the Millie story. I recalled Dennis while I was trying to help Millie. I'd tried other approaches in situations like this, some of which seemed at the time to be more clever but none of which worked as well. My attitude with Dennis was different too. In other difficult situations like this, I had tried the approach of competing in a battle of wits, or making sure I held the line without being taken advantage of, or striving to be the tougher opponent, but I never wound up sticking with any of those strategies. The approach with Dennis turned out to be the strongest one. A position of strength in tough conversations works that way. It's how we're wired.

CHAPTER 6

Take It Away!

Tough conversations can be pivotal opportunities for us and for those who engage with us. They can be turning points in a relationship or a life. Embracing tough conversations in a strong, confident, hopeful spirit empowers us to freely give and receive the rich blessings that these opportunities offer.

Tough conversations are pivotal in the sense that they can cause good or harm. They can provide healing or inflict injury. They can introduce new breakthroughs or new obstacles. They can tear down walls or build them up in relationships of all kinds—from children in school to heads of state—in marriages, friendships, or the workplace—in governments, churches, or businesses. Tough conversations are pivotal in the sense they can produce transformative growth or devastating destruction. Every human being engages in tough conversations at some point in life. Most people face them many times.

An important factor in the outcome of a tough conversation is how the participants feel about it before entering into it—how they feel about the specific encounter, and how they feel about tough conversations in general. What kind of attitude do they bring to tough conversations? And what kind of heart?

Let's start with attitude. The strongest attitude for approaching a tough conversation is to see it as an opportunity to achieve a resolution, breakthrough, or transformation that cannot be achieved any other way.

Take confrontation for example. We hear people say, "I don't like confrontation" or "I try to avoid confrontation" or "I believe avoiding confrontation is the right thing to do. I think people should live in peace." But avoidance is not the same as peace. There are times when confrontation is the only vehicle for achieving peace that lasts—peace based on truth and mutual respect.

Let's move to two other questions: What kind of heart is strongest for these challenging encounters? What kind of heart complements the strongest attitude?

We have gained plenty of knowledge from human history as well as personal experience about what doesn't work. We have learned that hate doesn't work. We have learned that fear doesn't work any better. We've seen plenty of attempts based on selfishness, and those produce bad results too partly because selfishness tends to connect with fear. These approaches fail because they come from a heart of weakness instead of a heart of strength. In fact, the results of approaches based on hate, fear, and selfishness are so consistently bad that it stirs our curiosity about what the opposite approach would look like.

The opposite approach comes from the opposite kind of heart—a heart of strength, a heart that works for the way we're wired. This is the heart of Jesus—the heart of God, who created us in His image and wired us for strength. All we have to do to be strong is use the wiring He gave us.

In this book, I have discussed how the heart of Jesus works in tough conversations—what drives it and what it looks like. While my own frequent failure to emulate the heart of Jesus is embarrassing, I've learned valuable lessons from my failures as well as my successes. I have learned that the more I apply the heart of Jesus to tough conversations, the more I succeed in them. The less I apply His heart, the more I fail. When I talk about my successes or failures in tough conversations, I don't mean in the sense of a perfect outcome but in the sense of maximizing whatever potential the encounter provided.

Why did I focus on the heart of Jesus in a book about tough conversations? For two reasons. The first is a spiritual reason, and the second is a worldly one.

On a spiritual level, I'm thoroughly convinced by the evidence that Jesus was who He said He was—the incarnate God, the Son of God. That is the easiest claim imaginable to disprove if it were not true. I am convinced by the worldly evidence to which worldly logic can be applied. I am also convinced by the spiritual evidence that we experience as individuals.

The second reason is based purely on tangible reality. In the measurable context of human history, Jesus is the most influential man who ever lived. He has provided more positive influence than anyone else. His teaching has been revered more than the teaching of anyone else. He is admired more than anyone else. Not unanimously, just more than anyone else.

No matter how diligently we apply the heart of Jesus to our lives—no matter how sincere we are about living the heart of God—we'll never do it perfectly because in our mortal lifetime there will always be interference. We will never live the heart of Jesus perfectly, and we will never conduct all our tough conversations flawlessly. But at least we will have an approach to tough conversations in which we can feel strong, confident, calm, peaceful, and hopeful.

Of the ideas I have discussed in this book that relate to tough conversations with the heart of Jesus, here are six that have meant the most to me.

1. Embrace the opportunities of tough conversations.

I began this chapter by saying that tough conversations can be pivotal opportunities. I feel stronger in a tough conversation when I think in terms of opportunity instead of anxiety. Reflecting on the heart of Jesus helps me to anticipate the encounter as an opportunity for redemption, restoration, positive influence, forgiveness, breakthroughs, and transformation. It offers hope that someone's life, perhaps even my own, will be better off after the conversation than it had been before.

2. The right heart for tough conversations is more important than the right skills, because the right heart makes the right skills easier and more natural.

This idea helps me to focus more specifically on what the heart of Jesus is really about. The heart of Jesus is itself transformative, so it's a wonderful source for the right energy and confidence to bring to a tough conversation.

I also want to bring to the encounter the skills this book has described, but the heart is the force behind the skills. Learning the heart of Jesus is an endeavor we will never fully master in our mortal lifetime, but it is the most enriching experience we will ever know. When we look at the heart of Jesus, we are looking at the heart of God. The next four ideas relate to how we can apply the heart of Jesus to tough conversations.

3. **One of the most encouraging truths we have about tough conversations is that we are already wired to do them right because we are wired the same way Jesus is.**

This is a mind-blowing piece of information, and God doesn't waste any time telling us about it in His Word. The first chapter in the Bible tells us, "So God created man in His own image, in the image of God He created him; male and female He created them" (Genesis 1:27).

God wants us to understand this, and He is emphatic in the way He says it. He repeats Himself lest there be any doubt at all.

This means we function at our highest level of performance and effectiveness when we emulate Jesus— the Son God sent to show us the way.

We aren't wired so that we *have* to emulate Jesus. We are designed so that we feel stronger and more satisfied emotionally and spiritually when we *do* emulate Him. Emulating Him begins by focusing on His heart, and the Bible teaches us how to do this.

Some of the information about how we're created to lead the most successful, powerful, and satisfying lives by God's standards is so startling that many people reject it as being simply impossible. Yet they are the words of the One who created us, and He has our best interests at heart. Every word spoken by Jesus came directly from God His Father. Those words include the following statements from the Beatitudes.

> Blessed are the meek, for they will inherit the earth. (Matthew 5:5)

> Blessed are the merciful, for they will be shown mercy. (Matthew 5:7)

> Blessed are the pure in heart, for they will see God. (Matthew 5:8)

> Blessed are the peacemakers, for they will be called sons of God. (Matthew 5:9)

This is the heart Jesus displayed for us to emulate—the heart He gave us—the heart that provides the best life if we have the courage to trust it. The surprise is what powerful strength, courage, and confidence these qualities of the heart produce. This is the kind of heart that produces the best results in a tough conversation.

The next three ideas take this one further.

4. **The key to achieving the best results in tough conversations is to focus on the needs, well-being, and dignity of the other person and let your own needs, well-being, and dignity take care of themselves—and trust that they will.**

We're designed so that we are at our best and strongest when we're focused on the well-being of others, and we're at our worst and weakest when we focus on our own well-being. This is the heart that provides us with our greatest position of strength—in tough conversations and in life. The heart of Jesus always gives us the position of strength.

Many verses in the Bible said by Jesus or written by those He taught echo this idea in a variety of ways. Here's a recap of a few I have found most helpful for tough conversations.

> Be kind and compassionate to one another, forgiving each other, just as in Christ God forgave you. (Ephesians 4:32)

> Be completely humble and gentle; be patient, bearing with one another in love. (Ephesians 4:2)

> ... speaking the truth in love ... (Ephesians 4:15)

> Bear with each other and forgive whatever grievances you may have against one another. (Colossians 3:13)

> Carry each other's burdens, and in this way you will fulfill the law of Christ. (Galatians 6:2)

> Do nothing out of selfish ambition or vain conceit, but in humility consider others better than yourselves. Each of you should

> look not only to your own interests, but also
> to the interests of others. (Philippians 2:3–4)

> Therefore encourage one another and build
> each other up. (1 Thessalonians 5:11)

5. The heart of Jesus gains much of its strength from the fruits of the Spirit.

"The fruit of the Spirit is love, joy, peace, patience, kindness, goodness, faithfulness, gentleness, self-control" (Galatians 5:22). As with the Beatitudes, we are wired that focusing on these fruits of Jesus' Spirit that He longs to share with us creates our strongest inner state for tough conversations as for life.

6. Love conquers fear.

God has created us so that godly love conquers fear. Love is where our strength comes from, while fear is where our weakness comes from. A spirit of love provides strength for tough conversations.

> There is no fear in love. But perfect love
> drives out fear. (1 John 4:18)

> Fear of man will prove to be a snare, but
> whoever trusts in the Lord will be kept safe.
> (Proverbs 29:25)

> Love is patient, love is kind. It does not
> envy, it does not boast, it is not proud. It

is not rude, it is not self-seeking, it is not
easily angered, it keeps no record of wrongs.
Love does not delight in evil but rejoices
with the truth. It always protects, always
trusts, always hopes, always perseveres.
Love never fails. (1 Corinthians 13:4–8)

What made Jesus strong in His love was that He gave
it to those who loved Him and those who hated Him.
His love was selfless, and selfless love can be a powerful
source of transformation in tough conversations.

Tough conversations offer so much opportunity!
They can be a vehicle for healing instead of hurt, for
transformation instead of destruction. Think of how many
people look back on a well-conducted tough conversation
with gratitude. What if we could anticipate these
encounters with gratitude as well by thinking of them as
gifts instead of burdens?

We have been given so much potential to use tough
conversations for positive transformation. We have been
given instruction for developing the right heart for tough
conversations from the very Creator of that heart. And
He's wired us to get it right if only we use the instruction
He has provided.

The principles that enable us to succeed in tough
conversations are the same ones that enable us to succeed
in life. God has given us the gift of love to conquer fear and
anxiety. He has also given us the gift of His Word and His
Son to show us the way.

The heart of Jesus provides exactly the right kind
of strength for tough conversations so we can approach

those situations with the anticipation of achieving breakthroughs that cannot be achieved any other way. Tough conversations are blessings for which we can be thankful if we approach them with the heart of Jesus.